The pathologies of the contemporary left, including cancel culture, are all too real and self-sabotaging. But they tend to be denied by those suffering from such afflictions, exploited by conservative enemies as a means to undermine the left, or pounced upon by ostensible friends as supposed evidence of the need for the left to take a conservative cultural turn. With his customary wit and logic, however, Burgis carefully navigates between the Scylla, Charybdis—and whatever a third maritime monster would be if this Greek mythological cliché came in a three-pack—of these ruinous responses. I just hope he doesn't get cancelled himself for writing this utterly essential book.

Leigh Phillips, co-author of *The People's Republic of Walmart: How the World's Biggest Corporations are Laying the Foundation for Socialism*

Ben Burgis provides a brutally honest and undeniably important critique of the left in this book. He rightly calls for a critical moment of self-reflection and strategy, making his book mandatory reading for serious leftists who want to accomplish their vision of a just world for workers beyond thought experiments and online activism. Burgis understands the importance of building a broader coalition on the left—one with less judgement and more emphasis on shared goals. By drawing on history, current events and his academic training in logic, Burgis provides a guide on how to make the movement more persuasive and appealing.

Ana Kasparian, producer and host at The Young Turks

Professor Ben Burgis has taught me how to question everything. He has sharpened my critical thinking. So imagine my

disappointment after finishing this book and finding absolutely nothing to question or criticize...It's fantastic! And I can't even count the number of times I reference it in conversation.
David Feldman, comedy writer, standup comedian, host of The David Feldman Show and co-host of The Ralph Nader Radio Hour

Ben Burgis knows we have a world to win, which is why he wants us in the newly reborn American left to be as effective and powerful as we can be. We can't build that power without abandoning the kind of vicious, exhausting, and downright mean behavior that so many of us have adopted towards our comrades and allies. Burgis makes the case here, in his trademark clear and readable style, for a much more politically serious—and much more personally pleasant—approach to building that movement. Who could be against that?
Micah Uetricht, managing editor of Jacobin and co-author of *Bigger Than Bernie: How We Go from the Sanders Campaign to Democratic Socialism*

Ben Burgis has recently emerged as one of the most insightful intellectuals of the democratic socialist left. In this essential new book, he turns his gaze on his own side, revealing and criticizing the underlying pathologies that prevent the American left from winning adherents, and, ultimately, winning power. Anyone seriously interested in creating a post-capitalist society must read this book.
Daniel Bessner, author of *Democracy in Exile: Hans Speier and the Rise of the Defense Intellectual*

Ben Burgis' *Canceling Comedians While the World Burns* is, appropriately enough, a very funny and stinging rebuke to some unhelpful strands of left-wing thinking and activism. With his characteristically accessible and down to earth style Professor

Burgis points out that winning the war of ideas isn't just about having the right ideas, but presenting them in a way that makes them appealing. This is something the left has been rather bad at over the past decades. This book gives one hope that things are changing.

Matthew McManus, author of *What is Post-Modern Conservativism: Essays on Our Hugely Tremendous Times*

Ben Burgis has written a wonderfully terse critique of some of the smelly little pathologies that plague the contemporary left. Using tight argumentation, one by one he dissects what exactly is problematic within trends such as the excesses of antifa, cancel culture, tankieism, privilege theory and a pervasive pseudo religious form of left moralism and how they are not only counterproductive, but positively harmful to any prospective project to reconstitute a socialist movement dedicated to increasing the power of the working class.

Ralph Leonard, Nigerian-British writer and cultural critic

Between runaway capital accumulation and levels of material inequality that might match or exceed any in human history, you might think socialists would be formulating strategies for material redistribution and closing in on taking power in real and meaningful ways. Instead, with honorable exceptions, the left continues to have difficulties building real institutional power, instead producing mean spirited and toxic subcultures, infused with HR politics and Silicon Valley algorithms. Ben Burgis has written a clarifying, humorous and sharp as hell wake up call for the left, and political culture at large. Read this book to get strategic about power and human about your fellow humans.

Michael Brooks, co-host of the Majority Report, host of The Michael Brooks Show, and author of *Against the Web: A Cosmopolitan Answer to the New Right*

Also by the author

Give Them an Argument, Zero Books, ISBN: 978-1-78904-210-8

With Conrad Bongard Hamilton, Matthew McManus and
Marion Trejo

Myth and Mayhem, Zero Books, ISBN: 978-1-78904-553-6

Canceling Comedians While the World Burns

A Critique of the Contemporary Left

Ben Burgis

Canceling Comedians While the World Burns

A Critique of the Contemporary Left

Ben Burgis

Winchester, UK
Washington, USA

JOHN HUNT PUBLISHING

First published by Zero Books, 2021
Zero Books is an imprint of John Hunt Publishing Ltd., No. 3 East St., Alresford,
Hampshire SO24 9EE, UK
office@jhpbooks.com
www.johnhuntpublishing.com
www.zero-books.net

For distributor details and how to order please visit the 'Ordering' section on our website.

Text copyright: Ben Burgis 2019

ISBN: 978 1 7890 4547 5
000 0 0000 000 0 (ebook)
Library of Congress Control Number: 2020942259

A CIP catalogue record for this book is available from the British Library.

Design: Stuart Davies

UK: Printed and bound by CPI Group (UK) Ltd, Croydon, CR0 4YY

We operate a distinctive and ethical publishing philosophy in
all areas of our business, from our global network of authors to
production and worldwide distribution.

Contents

To all of my friends and comrades in left media, in organizations like the Democratic Socialists of America, and even in some of the least dismal corners of academia who are helping to push back against the nonsense critiqued in this book and to create a smarter, funnier, and more strategic version of the left.

Acknowledgments

My editor Doug Lain patiently helped me brainstorm the idea for this book. At the end of the process, he told me it was an important enough intervention to be worth going ahead with if I was willing to "take the heat." Doug, Leigh Philipps, Matt McManus, and Mark Warren all made valuable suggestions about early drafts. My good friend and frequent collaborator Michael Brooks helped shape my understanding of some of the most important arguments presented here over the course of many, many conversations about these topics. Ryan Lake helped me crystalize many of these thoughts during conversations at various Atlanta area Waffle Houses which mostly consisted of my ranting and Ryan making insightful comments. My wife Jennifer isn't obsessed with politics the way I am—and she isn't as much of a fan of problematic comedy as I am—but she was, as always, a constant source of love and support while I was writing this book. (Jennifer is enough of an animal-lover that she would be rightly annoyed with me if I forgot to mention that our dog, Lucy, and our cat, Shabazz, are also pretty awesome on the "love and support" front.) My *Dead Pundits Society* co-host Adam Proctor and my fellow members of the extended "crew" of *The Michael Brooks Show* like David Griscom, Matt Lech, and Daniel Bessner have influenced my overall political perspective in many ways that I realize and probably lots of ways that I don't. The same is true of Bhaskar Sunkara and the rest of the team at *Jacobin*. Finally, I've been consistently honored and humbled by the support of my Patreon community. More than a few of the ideas presented in the book were originally hashed out in essays I wrote for my patrons and in our "Discord Office Hours" group voice chats. I'm not always sure that I deserve their support but I'm always grateful to have it.

1

Lenny Bruce Can't Save Us

In April 2020, the comedian Louis C.K. donated $2800 to the presidential campaign of Joe Biden. That itself was neither interesting nor surprising. C.K. seems to be a pretty boring centrist Democrat. In November 2016, when he was at the height of his popularity, he went on Conan O'Brian's show to give his analysis of the election: "If you vote for Hillary, you're a grownup; if you vote for Trump, you're a sucker; if you vote for anyone else, you're an asshole."

My politics are not C.K.'s politics. I enthusiastically supported Bernie Sanders in the Democratic primaries and I have long-term political horizons that go well beyond anything Bernie was talking about in that campaign. I'm a proud member of the Democratic Socialists of America. I was willing to entertain tactical arguments that leftists should vote for Hillary Clinton in swing states to stop Donald Trump but I recommended at the time that any voter who was planning to take this advice wear rubber gloves to the polls. C.K., on the other hand, told Conan O'Brian that he didn't even regard Hillary as a lesser evil. "I think she's great," he said. "I'd take her over anybody."

What *is* interesting is that the Biden campaign gave back the money. Historically, Biden hasn't been very picky about donors. In 2019 he infamously attended a fundraiser held by the founder of a fossil fuel conglomerate the day after he participated in a CNN Town Hall on climate change. During his decades in the Senate he raked in an enormous amount of cash from credit card companies headquartered in his home state of Delaware, even though he must have known this created at the very least the *appearance* of a conflict of interest when he championed a bill that made it harder for ordinary Americans in debt to those companies to declare bankruptcy. He drew the line at C.K. Why?

In 2017, C.K.'s fellow comedian Tig Notaro announced that she was cutting her ties with him and made a vague reference to allegations of sexual misconduct. Reports from several other female comedians then established that C.K. had a pattern of asking his female colleagues for permission to masturbate in front of them. Sometimes they thought he was joking. But then he would actually do it.

All of this raises some complicated questions about consent. These women weren't his co-workers or subordinates. As standup comics, everyone involved was essentially a self-employed small businessperson. But some of them may have been sufficiently intimidated by his fame or eager for him to support their careers that they went along with behavior that made them deeply uncomfortable. It would be hard to imagine anyone thinking these factors were sufficient to make meaningful consent impossible if C.K. had asked a less successful female comedian out on a date and they'd started a conventional romantic and sexual relationship, so it's reasonable to wonder whether at least some of the way that the incident was received has less to do with well-thought-out norms about consent than the fact that C.K.'s particular kink was an unusual one that most people find distasteful. On the other hand, I can't deny that my own gut instinct here is to think that what he did was indeed fairly "problematic."

Still, *whatever* you make of this tangle of ethical issues, the bottom line is that Louis C.K.'s sins involved masturbation. Joe Biden was one of the loudest voices on the Democratic side of the aisle calling for the invasion of Iraq in 2002 and 2003. Well over a million human beings died in that conflict. In a sane world, Louis C.K. would have been the one who would have worried about people associating him with Joe Biden.

Biden having done something unfathomably worse doesn't excuse anything C.K. did. But the fact that the Biden campaign was clearly worried about how Democratic voters would feel about the donation tells us something about how seriously many American liberals and leftists take the business of morally evaluating comedians.

At least C.K. was "canceled" because of something he *did* outside of his comedy sets. Dave Chappelle is reviled by many progressives for doing exactly what comedians are supposed to do. He explored the ambiguities of hot button social issues by telling jokes.

Chappelle kicks off his 2019 special *Sticks and Stones* by singing a bar from Kendrick Lamar's "DNA" ("You mothafuckers can't tell me nothing/I'd rather die than listen to you..."). After a couple of stories and a little bit more singing, he pivots to the meat of the special, telling the audience that he's going to do two impressions. The first is of "the Founding Fathers of America when the Constitution was being written":

"Hurry up and finish that Constitution, nigger! I'm trying to get some sleep."

Before the second one, he tells the audience that they'll have to guess who it is:

"Duh...hey...der...if you do anything wrong in your life and I find out about it, I'm going to try to take everything away from you. And I don't care when I find out. It could be today, tomorrow, 15, 20 years from now, if I find out, you're fucking finished."

After the crowd shouts out a few guesses, he tells them, "That's right. That's *you*! That's what the audience sounds like to me."

The point here isn't exactly subtle. When Chappelle's eponymous show was airing on Comedy Central in the early 2000s, his most memorable skits included one skewering the Bush Administration for lying about Iraq, one about reparations, and a role-reversal skit about the two-tiered justice system that brutalizes poor black people for committing petty crimes while giving rich white bankers and Enron executives a slap on the wrist. Later in *Sticks and Stones* he goes out of his way to talk about his support for various liberal causes. If the point of the second "impression" was to signal that he was going to be telling a lot of jokes about what's often called "cancel culture," the point of the first one—a pretty unmistakable middle finger to the sensibilities of conservatives who revere the Founding Fathers—was to remind the audience that he was going to be satirizing cancel culture from a perspective still located firmly within their side of the political spectrum.

Many of Chappelle's critics either missed this point or decided that this was a distinction without a difference. They consistently interpreted the jokes in *Sticks and Stones* in the most uncharitable possible way.

The special does contain some fairly edgy humor. In one bit, he cheerfully describes himself as a "victim-blamer," saying that when he heard that Michael Jackson had allegedly molested children, his first reaction was to ask, "What were they wearing?" Besides, he suggested, Jackson's alleged victims had been lucky. He speculated that more than half of the audience had been molested but "it wasn't by no goddamn Michael Jackson, was it?"

A few critics had a sufficiently tone-deaf and literalistic reaction to that joke that one wonders if they knew they were watching a comedy special, but most of the ire directed at Chappelle both in the ocean of tweets that called him "garbage," "hot garbage," "transphobic garbage," and so on and in the reviews that trashed *Sticks and Stones* at publications like *Vice* and *Salon* focused on a joke about what's sometimes called "transracialism."

This issue came to widespread public attention in 2015 when Rachel Dolezal, who had until then been the head of the Spokane, Washington chapter of the NAACP, was outed by her parents as having been born white. Her parents were extreme right-wing evangelical Christians who thought the issue was a very simple one. Rachel was *pretending* to be black. Many liberals and leftists agreed with this analysis. Rachel herself insisted that her racial identification was sincere and deeply felt.

Chappelle doesn't mention Rachel Dolezal in his routine. His joke is about the idea of a black man like him being Chinese "inside." But comedy reviewers and social media users who thought *Sticks and Stones* was transphobic apparently took the point of the joke to be the same one that's been made by those social conservatives who seized on the Dolezal scandal to charge progressives with hypocrisy. They pointed out that the contemporary left strongly supports trans rights. We think that refusing to call someone by their preferred pronouns is deeply obnoxious, that forcing people to use restrooms that don't match the way they present themselves is despicable, and that laws against various forms of discrimination should include discrimination on the basis of gender identity. (I respond to the standard arguments against socially progressive positions on these issues in Chapter Two of my first book, *Give Them an Argument: Logic for the Left*.) And yet, these conservatives point out, many progressives thought that Dolezal was lying or guilty of "cultural appropriation" for saying she was black.

Here's the thing: *It really is hard to make sense of both positions without inconsistency.* The idea that "race" is more closely tied to biological characteristics than gender is fairly implausible. That doesn't mean, however, that the left is wrong to support trans rights. Just to be an annoying logic nerd for a second, the inference from "this combination of positions is inconsistent" to "one or more of the positions must be incorrect" is called *Reductio Ad Absurdum*. And the thing about *Reductio Ad Absurdum* ("reduction to absurdity") is that, while the discovery of such inconsistencies can be enough to alert you that your premises can't *all* be correct, it doesn't by itself tell you *which* premise you should go back and reject.

One possible response to an attempted *Reductio Ad Absurdum* is to show that you weren't being inconsistent after all by finding relevant disanalogies between the two issues on which you have seemingly inconsistent positions. Some people argued that the claim that Rachel Dolezal was "transracial" wasn't really like the claim that transgender people really have the gender identity they claim because transgender people typically experience their gender identity as involuntary. Others pointed out that people who claim a racial identity that diverges from that of their parents are far, far more rare than people who claim a gender identity that diverges from their biological sex and conclude that transracialism is, as Zeba Blay put it, "not a thing."

If you don't find such strategies for differentiating transracial from transgender identities promising, and you don't have a better strategy up your sleeve, you have two options. You can accept the socially conservative takeaway from this case or you can argue for exactly the opposite conclusion, as the black socialist scholar Adolph Reed does in his essay "From Jenner to Dolezal." Reed supports LGBTQ rights as a matter of course. He writes in another essay, "The Myth of Class Reductionism," that he knows of "no serious tendency on the left" that denies that prejudice against gay and trans people exists or that it's important to combat these attitudes. But in "From Jenner to Dolezal," Reed makes quick work of the alleged disanalogies just mentioned.

Transracism is "not a thing"? Why should the numbers matter? And even if they do matter for some reason, it's worth remembering that openly trans people used to be far more rare than they are now. Transwomen like Caitlyn Jenner don't have a choice? How could you possibly know that Rachel Dolezal doesn't experience her racial identity in the same way? Has she lied about other matters or strained her relationship with friends and relatives? Maybe so but that's between her and those friends and relatives. There's no reason her personal failings should automatically impeach the authenticity of her feelings about who she "really" is.

Reed's conclusion is not that we should go along with the social conservatives in accepting "essentialism" about both race and gender—you're black if and only if your parents were black, you're female as a matter of all the things "gender" can mean if and only if you're female as a matter of biological sex—but that we should reject it in both cases. Contrasting Dolezal with Caitlyn Jenner, whose then-recent gender transition made her a natural point of reference when Reed wrote the essay, he writes that advocates for racial and gender justice should not only accept Dolezal's right to an identity that diverges from biological essentialism about race but that they should admire her far more than they admire Jenner. Dolezal's journey led her to a "commitment to struggle for social justice." Jenner is a Republican.

Similar points were made in a paper written by Rebeca Tuvel, an untenured assistant professor of philosophy at Rhodes College, in an academic paper entitled "In Defense of Transracialism." That one angered so many people that a petition was circulated to demand that the journal, *Hypatia*, retract Tuvel's paper. As someone who shares Tuvel's profession (and academic discipline), I was horrified to see philosophy professors and graduate students reacting to a philosophical argument they didn't like not by writing papers of their own in response but by demanding that journal editors limit the range of acceptable discussion.

The open letter denounced "white cis scholars" who "engage in speculative discussion" without "engaging those scholars whose lives are most directly affected by transphobia and racism." Breaking it down into component parts, this means that Tuvel's sins were (a) not being black or trans, and (b) not engaging with relevant literature containing ideas or arguments she should have taken into account. The first of those complaints boils down to an appeal to what's sometimes called "standpoint epistemology," which is both dubious in itself and a dangerous game for the left to play. "Lived experience" doesn't automatically confer moral or political insight, Anyone who's seen right-wing Venezuelan emigres who supported Juan Guaidó's attempted coup accuse American leftists of "Venezuelasplaining to them," or right-wing Jewish people charging non-Jewish supporters of the Palestinian call to boycott Israel of anti-Semitism (and insisting that any attempt to refute this charge violated the principle that "Jews get to define anti-Semitism") should have realized by now that this game can be played in any number of directions. By contrast, (b) *could* be a legitimate criticism. If an academic writes a paper and a devastating objection to the core argument of that paper is already out there, it is indeed a problem for that argument. To establish that (b) is a compelling criticism in this particular case, you'd have to explain which ideas and arguments in the existing literature were relevant and persuasive, or at least sufficiently persuasive to make Tuvel's failure to respond to them a problem. In order to be rigorous and convincing such an explanation would have to take the form of *an academic paper responding to Tuvel's paper.*

Here's the thing: Whether or not this would be a justified complaint in this case, the idea that philosophy professors and graduate students would be moved to sign such an open letter by the failure of the author of some obscure academic article to sufficiently engage with relevant sources is an insult to the intelligence of everyone involved. Realistically, people are moved to that kind of action by the perceived violation of moral and political taboos, not by a suspicion that a paper published in an area that most signatories didn't even specialize in might have failed some test of academic rigor.

I was particularly disheartened to see the signatures of some people I know on the letter. Worse yet, some of them were, well, my kind of people—folks who read the left-wing magazine

Jacobin and who might have a rose emoji in their Twitter handles to signify that, like me, they're committed to a democratic socialist political perspective.

Of course, a standup comedy special is not an academic paper and the "cancelation" of Dave Chappelle in some quarters doesn't raise the same issues as an attempt to pressure a philosophy journal to retract an article. Even so, the common and thoughtless inference from "Dave Chappelle explored the uncomfortable analogy between racial and gender identity in a comedy special" to "Dave Chappelle is an anti-trans bigot" was depressing in some of the same ways.

Since a comedy special is not an academic paper, Chappelle didn't actually come to any sort of conclusion about the analogy, but he did send some pretty unsubtle signals that he isn't an opponent of trans rights. Immediately before the transracialism joke, he spent a few minutes riffing about what he imagines as points of tension between the different elements of the "LGBTQ" coalition, and in setting up *that* joke, he described their common struggle as being about overcoming "prejudice and discrimination." It's a safe bet that Dave Chappelle's stance on whether "prejudice and discrimination" are good things is "no."

Again: While I certainly don't think he was coming to a Moral Majority sort of conclusion about these matters, I wouldn't go so far as to claim that he was coming to the Reed/Tuvel conclusion either. Standup comedy specials that amount to well-worked-out arguments for clearly defined conclusions don't tend to be very funny. That's not what standup is *for*. It is, however, a good platform for comedians to think out loud about how they feel about complicated subjects. And it would be a shame if they had less room to do that because of anxiety that comedically exploring a fraught subject was going to be interpreted as an outright embrace of bad and reactionary conclusions about that subject.

To anticipate a standard response, I'm perfectly aware that scolding someone for telling an ambiguous joke is as much an expression of free speech as the joke itself. While free speech concerns *are* legitimate when cancel culture intersects with the semi-feudal structure of largely non-unionized American workplaces or the silencing powers of the corporate oligarchs who control so many tech platforms, that's not the issue here.

A different and better reason to dislike both the practice of moralistically policing the boundaries of acceptable comedy and a lot of the responses this practice inspires is that all of this is very bad for comedy as an art form. Nigerian-British socialist Ralph Leonard recently explored this in his essay "Dave Chappelle and Comedy."

I find myself in the weird situation of being against both dominant sides of the comedy wars. On the one side, you have the likes of Samantha Bee and Hannah Gadsby, with their *woke anti-comedy*, which is often very forced and contrived—obsessed with pushing the *right* political and ideological message. Play it safe instead of trying to engage with people—whether through humour or other means—and you will always end up sounding tediously unfunny, preachy and condescending.

However, the antithesis of the *woke* brigade isn't much better.

The anti-woke faction, drawn mainly from the alt-right, portray themselves as counter-cultural insurgents, who are reclaiming comedy from wokeness, yet their approach of *giving PC the middle finger* is very infantile. They think it makes them subversive and edgy to use words like *nigger* and *faggot* and make stupid jokes about immigrants and trans people, whom they see as the sacred cows of the liberal establishment. Their jokes are grating, unfunny and stale. I'm not outraged or offended by them. It takes a lot more than that to get me riled up. I just find their stuff boring.

In fact, it's gotten to the point where you often have to slog past the boring stuff to get to the good part of a *good* comedy special. When Bill Burr spends 10 minutes at the beginning of his otherwise brilliant 2019 special *Paper Tiger* talking about *how easily offended everyone is these days*, his irritation is too raw and his take is too simple for him to have anything funny to say about it. The special only gets good when he starts talking about himself. And Burr is an extraordinarily talented comedian who's only just now gotten to the point in his career when he's putting out his best stuff. Just try to imagine the stale, repetitive anti-SJW jokes you're going to get from the multitude of hacks and has-beens.

Leonard continues:

> I am of the George Carlin school of thought: you should be able to make a joke about absolutely anything. No subject should be taboo or have a metaphorical barbed wire fence around it—not race, rape, transgenderism, Islam, 9/11 or the Holocaust. No topic at all. It all depends on how the joke is constructed, how the hyperbole works and, more importantly, whether or not it is funny. If it is funny, does it have any depth to it?

I'm broadly sympathetic to this stance, although it's worth noting two things. First, while Carlin was in practice freewheeling enough about where he aimed his jokes that I see why Leonard attributes this principle to him, if you watch old clips of Carlin talking *about* comedy, he does express some reservations about "punching down." Second and more importantly, I think it's worth being cautious and realistic about the extent to which any of us completely know ourselves when it comes to any of this stuff. It's far too easy to delude yourself into thinking that *you* don't have any fenced-off areas because you have yet to hear anyone crack a joke about one of yours. Then again, when that *does* happen, a lot depends on how well the comedian pulls you in. Here's a small example of what I mean:

David Feldman has a long career as a standup and a comedy writer. He's written for everyone from Jon Stewart to Triumph the Insult Comic Dog. On the non-comedy side of his career, he's the co-host of *The Ralph Nader Radio Hour*. I've been lucky enough to be a regular guest on his solo podcast *The David Feldman Show*. This means that I regularly share episode lineups with another of David's regular guests, Jackie "the Joke Man" Martling, who was the main writer for Howard Stern back when I was in high school. When I started writing about politics, that's not a regular co-billing I would have predicted, but I get a big kick out of it.

David does *long* episodes, and the tone varies a lot from segment to segment. At the 2-hour mark, he might be yakking it up with Jackie—he does this thing where Martling will tell a particularly off-color joke and David will say "Jackie...no!" almost like he's in physical pain—but back at the 1 hour mark, when he's interviewing me about the differences between Bernie Sanders and Elizabeth Warren, he's deadly serious. In fact, David displays more unfiltered anger about injustices ranging from *de facto* racial segregation in the public-school system to the myriad ways that insurance companies screw over people trying to get life-saving medicine, than just about anyone else I know in left media. After a synagogue shooting—it says something deeply depressing about how many hate crimes and mass shootings there have been in the last few years that I can't remember *which* synagogue shooting—he wanted to ask me about gun control. He built up to his question like this:

"Look, I know that anti-Semitism will always exist..."

...and he paused for a perfectly timed beat before continuing:

"...as long as I do this show."

I'm sure the moment loses something in a description like this, but I found it hilarious at the time. I should add that while my family background is secular and ethnically mixed, part of that background is Ukrainian-Jewish. I inherited pretty stereotypically Jewish looks and I've had an anti-Semitic remark or two directed at me over the course of my life. It's not a frequent occurrence and it's not particularly traumatic, but it does happen and I've never found it particularly funny. Good comedy—or at least good comedy of a certain kind—works by seducing us into laughing at things that we normally think of as extremely unfunny in much the same way that good literature often seduces us into identifying with characters we'd disapprove of in real life. The function of good art is often to make our inner lives more interesting by making us extremely uncomfortable.

Getting mad at someone for *not* being seduced into laughing at taboo material is asinine. You might as well get mad at someone you have a crush on for not finding you attractive. But the less people worry about *whether it's OK* to search for humor in this or that fenced-off area and the more they worry about how to do so in a way that sucks us into laughing about it, the better comedy will be as an art form.

...which is exactly what it is. Comedy is a form of entertainment that, when executed with enough skill and vision to have a deeper effect than just eliciting a quick laugh in the moment, becomes a form of art.

What it isn't—any more than novels, movies, or prestige TV—is a *way of changing the world*. American progressives in particular have often had trouble with that distinction. Think about the way that legions of liberal or even radical viewers related to Jon Stewart and *The Daily Show* during the Bush years. Or the way that, in the Trump era, *The Marvelous Mrs Maisel* has revived the secular sainthood of Lenny Bruce. There's a deeply embedded idea in the American progressive imagination that comedians are bold important truth tellers who change society simply by speaking truth to power—the way a court jester can get away with telling the king that the peasants are starving.

One problem with this fantasy is that speaking truth to power is wildly overrated. By and large, the powerful know the truth. If you're worried about starving peasants, don't bother trying to appeal to the conscience of the king. If the king *had* a functioning conscience, he wouldn't be able to hold onto his throne in the face of rival aristocrats and scheming usurpers. You're better off organizing the peasants themselves into a militant movement for land reform.

On *The West Wing*, unscrupulous Republicans were always reduced to silence after they were dressed down in a particularly eloquent way by President Bartlett or some other speechifying liberal. (The memory of Joseph Welch's 1954 takedown of Joe McCarthy—"have you no decency sir at long last..."—looms large in his view of how politics works.) In the version of the fantasy on display in *The West Wing*, deadly serious politicos rather than disarmingly goofy court jesters are the ones somehow defeating powerful adversaries just by being *so damn good* at speaking truth to them, but the expectation that *something* along these lines would work was reflected in February 2016 when about a million heartbreakingly earnest liberals got way too excited about going on social media and sharing comedian John Oliver's 22-minute segment "Donald Trump." The most memorable part of the segment was Oliver's gleeful discovery that the original surname of Donald's ancestors had been "Drumpf." Seemingly convinced that the mere repetition of this name would have some sort of quasi-magical effect, legions of liberals spent *years* calling Trump "Drumpf." Sadly, it doesn't seem to have had any particular effect on the voters in the rustbelt swing states who sent "Drumpf" to the Oval Office. It's also worth noting that the anti-communist witch-hunts in which McCarthy initially played a major role lasted long after his iconic exchange with Jack Welsh. The main investigatory body wasn't the McCarthy-chaired Permanent Subcommittee on Investigations in the Senate but the House Un-American Activities Committee, whose prestige slowly declined as times changed, but which kept doing pretty much what McCarthy had been doing with gradually diminishing returns until 1975. Good rhetoric is important. We can't persuade people to come around to our side without it. But good rhetoric about the other side being bad, whether presented in a serious or a savagely funny way, doesn't actually do anything to make the bad people go away.

Another problem with this fantasy is that good comedians aren't necessarily good political commentators. Being able to be very funny about KFC Famous Bowls, or to do a hilarious impression of the speech patterns of George W. Bush—or even to do all that in a way that manages to convey something interesting about the human condition—doesn't mean you have any special insight into what's wrong with our society or how it can be fixed. This became painfully obvious on October 30, 2010, when Jon Stewart and his close collaborator Stephen Colbert actually managed to bring a couple hundred thousand fans of *The Daily Show* and *The Colbert Report* to march through the streets of Washington D.C. to *do something* about what ailed American politics. They didn't use this rally to talk about single-payer healthcare or rebuilding the crumbling labor movement or ending America's seemingly endless wars in the Middle East. Their big cause was...politeness.

Writing 9 years after Stewart and Colbert's "Rally to Restore Sanity," *The New Republic*'s Alex Shephard recites a litany of cringe-worthy details.

> Stewart's audience picked up on the message, carrying signs with messages like "I disagree with you but I'm pretty sure you're not Hitler," and "Things are pretty OK," and "What do we want? Moderation!!! When do we want it? In a reasonable time frame."

The decision to make this an ostensibly nonpartisan affair led to a number of weird incongruities. Republicans were welcomed, but there were probably more conservatives on stage (thank you, Kid Rock) than in the audience…

Things were not "pretty OK" in 2010. They were in fact so not-OK that trends already well underway led a few years later to an openly racist reality television host becoming president by appealing to anti-establishment anger.

It's safe to say that none of this reflects well on Jon Stewart or Stephen Colbert. But here's a more basic question: Why would hundreds of thousands of people show up to a political rally organized by *comedians* in the first place?

Some social media users who put rose emojis in their Twitter handles to signal their allegiance to democratic socialism will get outraged about the content of Bill Burr's last Netflix standup special in such a deadly serious way that you'd think that Burr was running for a seat on the National Political Committee of the Democratic Socialists of America. This kind of thing is bad and embarrassing for at least four reasons.

First, it makes for shallow criticism. Puritans of all political and religious flavors tend to make lousy art critics for the simple reason that they read every poem as a manifesto and read every line of that "manifesto" in a dully literalistic way. Did Andres Serrano take a picture of a plastic crucifix drowning in his own urine? Well, it must mean that he HATES CHRISTIANITY SO MUCH HE WANTS TO PEE ON IT. If Bill Burr performs an angry rant about women in the context of a special largely devoting to both funny and painful reflections on his lifelong struggle with anger management, it must mean that HE'S TELLING HIS AUDIENCE EXACTLY WHAT HE REALLY THINKS ABOUT WOMEN. No need to think about any of it any more deeply than that.

Second, for all the reasons laid out so well by Ralph Leonard, it's bad for comedy as an art form. Third, it reflects a basic confusion about the difference between comedy and politics. Feeling betrayed when Dave Chappelle tells a joke that reveals that he doesn't share all of your moral and political values is the flip side of the same ridiculous coin as following your favorite late-night hosts through the streets of Washington D.C. holding a protest sign. The final problem, and the one most relevant to the overall thesis of this book, is that while online outrage mobs are pretty impotent when it comes to changing the larger world—Chappelle and Burr's careers will be just fine—those mobs *do* often succeed in making leftists look like humorless scolds. This needlessly alienates all the regular people watching from the bleachers.

I can almost hear some readers of the rose-emoji Twitter variety saying, "It *shouldn't* alienate them! People are dying because they can't afford insulin. Anyone who can't see that there are more important things at stake here than the fact that some leftists are annoying is worthless anyway."

And that reaction makes a certain amount of sense—*if* you don't really believe in changing the world, and deep down you see your politics as a symbolic performance, a way of "taking a stand" against an insurmountably powerful opposition. *Hey, at least I said something. And that makes me better than everyone who said nothing.*

If, on the other hand, you hold out hope that you might win— and really, if you've given up on that, what's the point?—then you need to think hard about how to appeal to regular people who don't spend all day every day reading and tweeting about politics. If someone rarely takes the time to reflect on their political beliefs, and they only happened to notice your existence when you were being a ridiculous scold, they're not going to stick around to notice all the good points that you make the rest of the time. Finding ways to get basically apolitical "normies" excited about fighting for a better world can be tricky under the best circumstances. I certainly don't claim to have all the answers. But I'm pretty certain that making ourselves look like overgrown hall monitors is unhelpful.

2

Scenes from a DSA Convention

The Democratic Socialists of America held their National Convention in Atlanta in August 2019. The day after the convention ended, Tucker Carlson played carefully selected clips from the proceedings on Fox News in order to portray the organization in the worst possible light.

In 2015, DSA had a few hundred members. The most recent figure I've seen in 2020 was 70,000. During this period of explosive growth, DSA has played an outsized role in promoting the two presidential campaigns of Bernie Sanders and putting "Medicare for All" at the center of the national political conversation. Its chapters have organized "brake light clinics" in which DSA members volunteer to swap the burned-out brake lights of passing drivers in order to minimize their interactions with the police. (It's become fashionable in some quarters of the left to mock this activity, but I love it. Such clinics amount to a useful form of street theater that builds goodwill in local communities, makes an understated but deadly serious point about the imbalance of power between ordinary working-class people and increasingly militarized police forces, and may actually save a life or two in the process. The left could use more of that kind of creativity, not less.) DSA members have also walked picket lines with striking workers, organized tenants to fight the power of landlords, helped undocumented workers resist deportation, and generally been present and accounted for everywhere that people are fighting for various kinds of social change that make the society around us at least slightly fairer and more equal. At the same time, instead of being content with such reforms, they've helped to revive long-dormant big ideas about how we could change our whole economic system to get at the root of many of these problems. So, yeah, the DSA? I'm a fan. But nothing I saw in Tucker's clips surprised me.

The first thing his viewers got to see was a speaker laying out a list of rules ranging from "no strong scents in the chill-out room" to a requirement that delegates—very few of whom, needless to say, were either deaf or fluent in American Sign Language—use "ASL applause" (i.e. wiggling their fingers) instead of actual applause in order to accommodate anyone in the room who may have some extremely rare condition making them especially sensitive to loud noises. The next clip features a delegate from California who starts with "hey guys" and launches into an angry lecture, haranguing the 1500 or so delegates about the problems posed to the noise sensitive by "whispering and cross-talk." Not to be outdone, an even angrier voice rings out from the crowd scolding the comrade from California for using "gendered language" ("guys"). Tucker has more clips ready, and more snickering to do.

That he's cherry-picked a few minutes spread throughout a long weekend goes without saying. Tucker Carlson is a toxic propagandist whose specialty is promoting the agenda of the anti-immigrant right by portraying the left as indifferent to the concerns of the American working class. He could have shown his viewers a few minutes of the fiery speech delivered to the convention by Cecily Myart-Cruz, the Vice President of United Teachers Los Angeles, who'd just helped lead 30,000 teachers out on strike for better pay and smaller class sizes with overwhelming support from the larger community. Or he could have thrown in a clip or two of delegates voting on a set of priorities for the next 2 years that included not only mobilizing for Bernie Sanders and continuing the campaign for Medicare for All but starting major new pushes on housing and childcare and for a Green New Deal that could create millions of well-paid public sector jobs and help to save the planet in the process. If Tucker had shown any of that, it would have ruined his narrative. So he didn't. But that's to be expected. You might as well get angry at a spider for building a web. What I find incomprehensible is the behavior of the people in the clips he *did* want to show. He didn't get this footage by sending spies into the convention with hidden cameras. *The DSA itself was streaming it.* Everyone knew this, and everyone seemed to think "we're building the kind of movement where no one is allowed to make a loud noise" was a good face to present to the world.

To anticipate a tedious but inevitable strawman, no one thinks accommodating the disabled is a bad thing. That's not the issue. You can engage in a reasonable level of accommodation informed by advice from qualified medical professionals without turning the dial up to 11 and acting as if there are no competing goals to weigh against the benefits of maximalist accommodation. The problem isn't even *just* that it was painfully obvious that none of the people we saw in the clips (or any of the off-screen organizers who went along with bizarre rules like "no clapping") so much as paused to consider how all of this would look to any viewers who weren't immersed in the subculture of the left. That's certainly *part* of the problem, but there's a deeper issue.

What Tucker's clips so perfectly captured was an unmistakable tone of scolding one-upsmanship. It was a race to see who could go the furthest in the direction of finding ways to prove their own moral virtue by finding ways to object to the utterly unremarkable behavior of their assembled comrades. This reeks of an "irl" ("in real life") version of the pathology of Left Twitter so memorably critiqued from the left in left-wing British cultural critic Mark Fisher's classic 2013 essay "Exiting the Vampire Castle."

The Vampires' Castle specializes in propagating guilt. It is driven by a *priest's desire* to excommunicate and condemn, an *academic-pedant's desire* to be the first to be seen to spot a mistake, and a *hipster's desire* to be one of the in-crowd.

If you've logged any serious amount of time in left spaces and you don't recognize anything you've seen in Fisher's essay, I envy you. I make no claims here about how widespread any of the attitudes or practices I'm critiquing may be. If fewer people are trapped in the Vampire Castle than I imagine, that's wonderful, but we should still work to free those few, especially considering that they're often the loudest and most visible representatives of our movement. If we want to get to the point where we could hope to win over a massive majority of the population to socialism, fighting the Vampire Castle is a strategic imperative. As Fisher says, the VC "doesn't know how to make converts. But that, after all, is not the point."

Instead, leftists who are in the grips of this way of doing things often treat the left like a clubhouse that needs to be guarded to make sure that no one who doesn't hold all the correct positions and know all the correct ways of speaking and acting gets to step inside. You can't act that way and become a movement *of* and not just *for* the working-class majority of society.

One of the oddest reactions I've gotten when I've told people that I'm writing a book called *Canceling Comedians While the World Burns* is, "Why do you think idiots yelling at comedians is important enough to write a book about?" or "Is cancel culture that big a deal? Don't you have higher political priorities?" The answer is yes—*and that's the point*. When outraged Romans charged Nero with "fiddling while Rome burned," they weren't saying that the annoying way the Emperor played his fiddle was more important than the fact that Rome was burning. They were saying that him playing the fiddle instead of doing something about the fire was a problem. But at least his fiddling wasn't making the fire worse. That's where the analogy breaks down. Even if you only spend a few minutes a day tweeting toxic bile at the Problematic and you devote a dozen hours a week to your DSA chapter's labor organizing working group, those few minutes a day contribute to giving outside observers a deeply

22

unappetizing impression of the left.

The larger subject of which "canceling comedians" is a representative example is a cluster of left pathologies that includes everything from the revival of "tankie" attitudes (i.e. kneejerk apologism for every authoritarian regime that makes use of socialist rhetoric and symbolism) to hysteria about minor political differences within the left to the bad habit of framing disparities between different groups primarily in terms of introspective psychodrama about "unearned privilege" (as if the absence of oppression were something that had to be *earned*). There are good arguments against all of these things in principle. What I'm most concerned to show in what follows, though, is that they're all symptoms of the failure of the contemporary left to think strategically instead of turning politics into a moral performance. In other words, I'm interested in convincing my friends and comrades to stop acting this way because I don't want us to *lose*.

This is not an "I'm a leftist but..." book. While I don't necessarily think the most fire-breathingly radical slogans that any element of the left puts forward on any given issue are always especially helpful, you're not going to find any particularly "heterodox" policy positions here.

My attitude is well represented by one of my favorite quotes from Christopher Hitchens. It comes from "Blunt Instruments" — an essay that "Hitch" wrote in the mid-1980s (i.e. about two-and-half decades before his own post-9/11 turn to the dark side).

I have never been able, except in my lazier moments, to employ the word "predictable" as a term of abuse. Nor has the expression *knee-jerk* ever struck me as a witty way of denigrating a set of strongly held convictions...Speaking purely for myself, I would be alarmed if my knee failed to respond to certain stimuli. It would warn me of a loss of nerve. I have written in the past year about the MX missile, constructive engagement, the confirmation of Edwin Meese and other grand guignol episodes. Naturally I hope that my arguments were original, but I would be depressed to think that anyone who knew me or my stuff could not easily have "predicted" the line I would take.

In the charmed circle of neoliberal and neoconservative journalism, however, "unpredictability" is the special emblem and certificate of self-congratulation. To be able to bray that "as a liberal, I say bomb the shit out of them," is to have achieved that eye-catching, versatile marketability that is so beloved of editors and talk-show hosts. As a lifelong socialist, I say don't let's bomb the shit out of them. See what I mean? It lacks the sex appeal, somehow. Predictable as hell.

I'm fully committed to the full range of predictable-as-hell leftist goals, from guaranteeing free abortion on demand as part of a comprehensive system of single-payer national health insurance to stopping America's endless wars in the Middle East to working toward the replacement of the existing economic order with some sort of democratic socialist system that treats workers not as tools for moving packages around Jeff Bezos' warehouses but as human beings with a right to a far greater level of control over their lives both on and off the job. I'm writing this book *because* I care about the same goals as the people I'm critiquing and I believe that their way of doing things is often deeply counterproductive.

Some leftists have a hard time hearing critiques of the "exclusive clubhouse" conception of the left without interpreting it as advocacy for "class reductionism," which they understand to be the position that socialists shouldn't bother with any political issue that isn't directly and obviously about economic class struggle. In my experience, accusations of "class reductionism" tend to be unfair caricatures of the positions held by the people to whom this label is applied, but I'm sure there are exceptions to this rule. (As Cicero said, there is no position so absurd that it hasn't been advocated by some philosopher.) At any rate, whoever else may or may not hold this view, it isn't an accurate representation of my position or of the historical tradition with which I identify. In addition to the struggles waged by workers against their bosses for higher pay, better working conditions, and more of a say on the job, socialists have *always* supported "non-economic" struggles to make the world more equal and less brutally hierarchical. Karl Marx supported the Irish Republicans fighting for independence from the British Empire. His daughters wore green ribbons in their hair to show their support for that struggle. (Contrary to the impression that you'd get from reading critiques of Marxist "eurocentrism" spread by academics who should know better, Marx was equally supportive of the sepoy mutineers who fired the first shots for the independence of India from Britain in 1857.) And any account of the early decades of the American Civil Rights Movement that doesn't include the socialist and communist parties in starring roles is more of a sanitized fairy tale than real history.

These commitments flow from both moral and strategic sources. For one thing, a lot of these allegedly "non-economic" battlefronts are pretty damn economic. The British didn't conquer India for the purpose of "culturally appropriating" its curry. As Barbara Fields famously put it, it's absurd to talk about the history of race relations in the United States "as though the chief business of slavery were the production of white supremacy rather than the production of cotton, sugar, rice, and tobacco." White supremacist attitudes might have taken on a life of their own in the subsequent centuries, but they came into existence to justify the financially lucrative practices of colonialism and slavery. Nor are contemporary "culture war" topics like the scope of anti-discrimination ordinances really separable from the economic class struggle. If your boss can fire you for being gay or trans or undocumented, you have a lot less power on the job.

Beyond that, socialists have always made a long-term strategic calculation that bigotry should be combated because it interferes with the unity of the working class. This is one reason why, as Adolph Reed points out in "The Myth of Class Reductionism," "Communists, Socialists, labor-leftists, and Marxists of all stripes" have historically been at the "forefront of struggles for racial and gender justice." On a slightly more abstract level, I have a hard time seeing the point of being a socialist in the first place if you aren't moved by the kind of broadly egalitarian and democratic impulses that would make you outraged by discrimination and prejudice and petty social cruelties.

My great-grandfather Morris Field was part of the founding leadership of the United Auto Workers (UAW) in the 1930s. He was also a member of Jay Lovestone's anti-Stalinist splinter faction of the American Communist movement (the Independent Communist Labor League), so great-grandpa's star had declined in the UAW for predictable reasons by the time the McCarthyite 1950s rolled around. My favorite story about him isn't one I heard growing up. I found it in August Meier and Elliot Rudwick's book *Black Detroit and the Rise of the UAW*. In June 1942, a small group of black workers were promoted to jobs previously only held by whites at a Detroit-area Dodge Truck plant. This sparked a racist walkout. The union "at once sent in Morris Field, Assistant Director of the UAW's Chrysler Division, who bluntly announced that 'the local will have to accept the negroes.'" Not exactly the St Crispin's Day Speech, but I still found that line heart-warming to read. I would have been disappointed and disgusted if Morris had been on the wrong side of history. Similarly, I'd hate the thought of any future great-grandson or great-granddaughter or non-binary great-grandchild of mine finding out that I'd taken the side of the bigots and bullies and idiots on any parallel issue.

...all of which is to say that when I talk about "the full range" of predictable-as-hell left-wing goals, I'm not just talking about the portion of the range having to do with workplaces and wealth redistribution. I'm also not interested in simply venting about those on the left whose behavior strikes me as an impediment to achieving those goals. I want to try to figure out *why* we're making these mistakes and how we might try to do better.

3

Decision Theory for the Left

In my first book, *Give Them an Argument: Logic for the Left,* I tried to make the case that left-wing activists should take the time to learn how to break down the logical structure of arguments and steer clear of logical fallacies. That book was intended to double as a polemic about the value of learning those things and a very basic introductory informal logic textbook in which I demonstrated how to use these tools by using them to refute the arguments of reactionary blowhards like Ben Shapiro.

Part of my case for learning this stuff had to do with the value of being able to debunk right-wing arguments. Part of it, though, was about how a failure to focus on getting our arguments right contributed to the pathologies of the contemporary left.

[A] left that *only* knows how to shame, call out, privilege-check, and diagnose the allegedly unsavory motivations of people who disagree with us will lose a lot of persuadable people whose material interests should put them on our side. What's more, left-wing people who really do share all the same long-term goals often find themselves disagreeing about strategy and tactics. Should we advocate a Universal Jobs Guarantee (UJG) or Universal Basic Income (UBI)? Or are all demands for radical reforms within the current system counterproductive distractions from the fight against capitalism itself? Should social democrats and socialists try to form a labor party? Can we take over the Democratic Party? Should we just focus on non-electoral activism? These are complicated questions. If we're out of practice using the kind of reasoning skills enhanced and sharpened by the study of logic, if we find that we're just *better* at privilege-checking and snark and diagnosing people's motivations than we are at making compelling arguments for our positions, the inevitable consequence is that when we argue with each other about these points of intra-left disagreement, all of those weapons are turned inward. That kind of thing makes the left about as appealing to potential converts as an endless Twitter war about race science with toxic right-wing logicbros. We can do better.

Like the argument I made in that passage, the critique of the left I'll be presenting here is based on strategic considerations. Before going any further it's worth taking a step back and thinking about the general structure of arguments about strategy.

In *Give Them an Argument*, I was able to nail down where my targets' reasoning went wrong in a relatively precise way. "This is this fallacy, that's that one." The strategic arguments I'll be making in the remaining chapters of this book necessarily involve a fuzzier element. A lot of my premises are going to involve judgment calls. Given the nature of the subject that's probably unavoidable. It also means you might decide you disagree with me about some of this stuff not because you disagree with my goals but because you weighed all the same evidence I did and you made a different call.

That said, we can at least be analytically rigorous about pinning down when judgment calls need to be made and how they enter into larger chains of reasoning. To put it differently, we can be precise in thinking about how and in which ways reasonable leftists who share the same goals can rationally and fruitfully disagree. I'll devote the rest of this chapter to laying out the basics of that framework and giving a real-life example of how it can be applied to an intra-left political controversy.

Let's start with a couple of quick distinctions. (If you read *Give Them an Argument*, some of this will be familiar to you. Be patient—the new stuff is coming soon!) Logic is the study of arguments. *Deductive* logic is the branch of logic where we examine arguments to see if they're "valid" — i.e., if the structure of the argument makes it impossible for the premises to be true without the conclusion being true. A "sound" argument is a valid argument with all true premises. Take this simple syllogism:

Premise One: All dogs are animals.
Premise Two: My miniature schnauzer Lucy is a dog.
Conclusion: Lucy is an animal.

Someone who agrees with Premise One *and* Premise Two but disagrees with the conclusion is being inconsistent. They can't be right about all three statements. And both premises are obviously true. This is the best position we can be in as far as arguments go. We know that the premises are all true, and we know that they *deductively entail* the conclusion (i.e. we know that the argument is valid), so we know that the conclusion must be true too.

Sadly, the universe is often frustratingly uncooperative with our inquiries. It gives us incomplete and ambiguous evidence, and the relationship between that evidence and any particular conclusion we want to draw often falls short of the gold standard of deductive validity. "Inductive logic" is the branch of logic where we're examining arguments to see if they're inductively "strong." A strong argument is one where, if we believe the premises to be true, the logical relationship between the premises and the conclusion gives us a *good reason* (that falls short of certainty) to believe that the conclusion is true. This is a matter of probability. Deductive validity is binary. An argument is valid or invalid, the way a standard light switch is either set to "on" or "off." Inductive strength comes in degrees. Some strong arguments might make a good reasoner 60 percent sure that the conclusion is true. Others might make that good reasoner 99 percent sure.

The branch of inductive logic that's relevant to *strategic* arguments is called "decision theory." This in turn revolves around the concept of "expected value." You get expected values from combining probabilities with utilities. You can think of the utility of an outcome as how much we care about bringing it about—or, for negative utilities, how much we care about avoiding it.

I know that last paragraph was fairly abstract and that it included a lot of new terminology. If you don't feel like you quite know what any of it means yet, don't worry! We'll unpack it slowly. (Conversely if you're a big ol' logic nerd who already knows all of this, be patient for just a little bit longer and we'll start connecting the dots.) To see how probabilities and utilities come together in decision theory, let's start with a simple mathematical example. If you're the kind of reader that starts itching when you see the word "mathematical," rest assured that this is the only such example in this book! And if your reaction is not just to itch but to go into full-on mathphobic panic mode, feel free to skip the next few paragraphs. (I'm tempted to make a joke about trigger warnings here but I'll resist the temptation.)

Let $P(O)$ be the probability of some outcome O and $U(O)$ be its utility. Someone invites you to play a coin-flipping game. If the coin comes up heads, you have to give the other person $1. If it comes up tails that person has to give you $2. Let's assume that it's a fair coin, so the two outcomes are equally probable. Further assume that the only kind of utility we care about in this case is financial—the positive utility of $2 for the tails outcome and the negative utility of $1 for the heads option. (Note that probabilities are always on a scale from 0 to 1. You can represent utilities with any numbers you like as long as you're being consistent about it.) In this example, there are only two possible outcomes—O_1 and O_2. Here are their probabilities:

$P(O_1)=.5$

$P(0_2)=.5$

To get the expected value of playing the game, just multiply the probability of each possible outcome by its utility and then add it all up. That gets you:

$$[P(O_1) \times U(O_1)] + [P(O_2) \times U(O_2)] = [(.5) \times (2)] + [(.5) \times (-1)] = (1) + (-.5) = .5$$

Remember that in this case the utility represents a dollar amount (50 cents). What this "expected value" means concretely is that decision theory tells you that if someone offers you a chance to play this game you should go for it—as long as the entry fee is less than 50 cents.

More interesting cases—like all the ones about political strategy in this book—involve kinds of utility too complicated for this kind of precise number-crunching to be possible. Still, it's useful to start with *one* example where the probabilities and utilities can actually be quantified so we can see exactly how probabilities, utilities, and expected values are supposed to fit together.

Note too that this theory can be treated either in the way that I do above, as a *normative* theory (i.e. a theory of how we rationally "should" act) or as a *descriptive* one (i.e. a theory of how people do act). One of the fundamental assumptions of neoclassical economics (i.e. what you were taught if you ever took an Econ 101 class) is that decision theory is an accurate descriptive theory of how buyers and sellers actually act in markets—or at least that it's close enough to being accurate to be a useful predictive model.

You'll sometimes find economists (or libertarians who are fond of using vocabulary drawn from economics) talking about "revealed preferences." Anyone who talks this way subscribes to an extreme form of the descriptive version of decision theory. They think that everyone really does reason in the way that decision theory tells them to reason all the time. According to this view, what you *say* about your preferences doesn't reveal your "real" preferences. Instead, we need to look at your buying and selling behavior. So for example you might *say* that you care more about not getting cancer than you do about the taste of some potentially carcinogenic product, but if you know there's a high probability that it will give you cancer and you continue to buy it anyway, you must "really" assign a much lower negative utility to getting cancer than you say you do.

This is what can most charitably be described as a pretty silly assumption. For one thing, you've probably never done an expected value calculation in your life, so the idea that there's even a *pretty good* match-up between the results of such calculations and your actual decision-making (economic or otherwise) might seem pretty dubious. For another, pretty much every psychological study that's been done in the last several decades has been a new reminder of all the ways in which humans can be irrational, so the idea that we're all perfectly rational all the time seems...well...*unlikely* to be true. (It's often been hard to replicate psychological studies, but even if this "replication crisis" only left 10 percent of studies of human irrationality intact that would still be a mountain of evidence.) And even if we didn't have the benefit of knowing about empirical psychology, about 5 seconds of reflection on the cancer case should be sufficient to tell you that there's a world of difference between "knowing" something in the sense of being aware in the abstract that it's true but not thinking about it very much and "knowing" something in the sense of having deeply internalized the knowledge. That should be one clue about one of many ways in which economic and other kinds of decision-making can often be *wildly* irrational. If all of this makes you suspicious of the neoclassical economists' claims, rest assured that you're in good company. Lots of heterodox economists of various stripes agree with you.

None of this, though, does much to undermine decision theory as a normative theory of how we *should* make decisions when we have the knowledge and the leisure to use these logical tools to think hard about probability and utility. To see how such considerations can be applied to left political strategy, think about the controversy about Bernie Sanders' decision first to go on Joe Rogan's wildly popular YouTube show and podcast The Joe Rogan Experience and then to accept Rogan's "endorsement" of him.

Even as I'm writing this, enough has happened in the last few months that this seems like ancient history. To briefly review, Rogan's "endorsement" of Sanders consisted of the following comment which Rogan made after a guest (the rather odious right-wing hack Bari Weiss) asked him who he was going to vote for:

> I think I'll probably vote for Bernie. Him as a human being, when I was hanging out with him, I believe in him, I like him, I like him a lot. What Bernie stands for is a guy who—look. You could dig up dirt on every single human being that's ever existed if you catch them in their worst moment and you magnify those moments and you cut out everything else and only display those worst moments. That said, you can't find very many with Bernie. He's been insanely consistent his entire life. He's basically been saying the same thing, been for the same thing for his whole life. And that in and of itself is a very powerful structure to operate from.

Joe Rogan may be the most popular podcaster in the world. Part of the reason why is that he's at least as interested in marijuana and psychedelics and Mixed Martial Arts and standup comedy and a handful of other subjects as he is in politics of any kind. And when he does talk politics, his positions can best be described as "all over the place." He's progressive on some issues, reactionary on others, somewhat prone to conspiracy theories, and *very* prone to agreeing with whatever guest happens to be joining him in his studio at any given time. (He wouldn't be nearly as popular if he weren't so damn amicable.) His show appeals to many millions of young people (mostly young men) of varying shades of political belief, including millions who are relatively apolitical. As such, it was pretty obvious to anyone with any familiarity with Rogan and the reach of his show that his heartfelt praise for Sanders had the potential to give the Senator's campaign a nice boost about a week before the Iowa Caucus. Unsurprisingly, the Sanders campaign tweeted out the YouTube clip of Rogan's praise.

The words you hear Rogan saying at the beginning of that clip about how anyone's worst moments can be dug up and strung together to create a narrative about them predicted what happened next with pinpoint accuracy. Detractors of Sanders and Rogan went through a decade or so of the show's archives and Rogan's tweets and found both genuine instances of Rogan—who by his own cheerful admission is stoned out of his mind a fair amount of the time he's on air—saying offensive things and more dubious clips in which he's saying things that sound a lot more offensive when they're out of context. In one particularly remarkable example, he tells a bigoted joke and then immediately—literally a few seconds later—follows it up with an expression of regret ("that was a racist thing for me to say") and starts to backpedal. Needless to say, most of the angry OMG I CAN'T BELIEVE THAT BERNIE SANDERS WOULD TOUT AN ENDORSEMENT FROM THIS DISGUSTING MAN tweets that included the clip of him telling the joke ended before the expression of regret.

Much of this controversy was generated in bad faith by Bernie Sanders' political opponents. What I found interesting and disturbing, though, was that more than a few socialists and Sanders supporters joined in the condemnation. This drove me and my friend Michael Brooks to co-write a *Jacobin* article about the endorsement. Since we believed that Bernie Sanders was the candidate with the best chance of beating Donald Trump in the general election, we made a simple strategic argument.

Every successful presidential campaign is by definition a coalition of voters who don't agree with each other about everything but are willing to get behind a given candidate and their platform. The question is whether we're so allergic to having people in our coalition who haven't yet reached progressive positions on every issue that we're willing to risk losing what is arguably the most important election of our lifetimes.

Which is more important—stigmatizing Rogan for his bad views by refusing to make any welcoming gestures when he expresses interest in joining our coalition, or shutting down Donald Trump's concentration camps?

To see how decision theory can clarify the structure of strategic arguments, think about how and why someone who shared our goals might disagree with our judgment call in this case. First, they could worry that more voters could be turned off by Rogan's semi-endorsement than drawn to Sanders by it. In other words, they could point to a possible outcome of the decision to accept the endorsement that Michael and I neglected in our article. I wouldn't find that objection very compelling for the simple reason that this possible outcome struck me then and continues to strike me now as deeply improbable. Bluntly, I think that there are a hell of a lot fewer American voters (even in the context of a Democratic primary) who harbor such ultra-woke attitudes that they would be *less* likely to vote for someone "endorsed" by a semi-problematic podcaster and comedian like

Joe Rogan than there are voters who are fond of Rogan.

Alternately, they might grant that publicizing Rogan's praise at least slightly increased Sanders' chance of first becoming the Democratic nominee and then beating Donald Trump in November but thought it wasn't worth it given whatever utility could plausibly be brought about by progressives shunning people who talk and joke the way that Rogan sometimes does. Consideration of this possible objection is helpful for two reasons. First, it helps clarify the shape of the debate. To have a good decision-theoretic objection to "touting" the Rogan endorsement, it wouldn't be enough to think that socially ostracizing the Problematic has at least *some* positive utility. (I have my doubts about even this for reasons I've already indicated, but let's put that to one side for the moment.) You'd have to argue that some sufficiently probable outcome of the shunning strategy has *so much* utility that it outweighs an increased probability of an outcome that presumably has massive disutility from our perspective—a second Trump term. Bluntly, I doubt that very many of Sanders' left-wing critics would go along with *that*.

Of course, you might think that this framework for thinking about left strategy is too cold-bloodedly utilitarian. Aren't there such things as principles—lines we wouldn't cross even if crossing them had tremendous strategic value?

Sure. But decision theory can accommodate that too. Imagine a coin-flipping game where "heads" meant that you got $1000 and "tails" meant that your children would be sold into slavery. Presumably it wouldn't matter if we raised the payoff of heads to a million dollars or a billion dollars or however much money is currently in Jeff Bezos's bank account. One way of decision-theoretically modeling this idea is to say that the "tails" outcome in this game has *infinite* negative utility.

I don't deny that lines of principle of this kind exist. But I am inclined to think that if you see uncrossable lines like that *everywhere*, you probably need a new map.

Here's a plausible case of such a line: The setting is South Africa in the 1980s. You're a member of uMkhonto we Sizwe ("Spear of the Nation"), the armed wing of the African National Congress, and you've been captured by the apartheid government. The official who interrogates you offers you a deal for clemency if you rat on your comrades. We could doubtless fill in the details of the thought experiment in such a way that there's a utilitarian case to be made for taking the deal. (Maybe the comrades you're preparing to turn in are much less important than you are to the movement. Maybe no one knows you've been arrested so word of your betrayal won't get around and demoralize other comrades. Etc.) Even so, as a matter of principle you assign such a tremendous negative utility to informing to the enemy that you don't do it. Fair enough. Now, consider an American leftist in 2020 thinking about whether to tweet about why they found some standup comedy special horribly problematic. If you think that uncrossable lines of principle are likely to be found anywhere in *this* vicinity, your map is so inaccurate and unhelpful that you should set it on fire.

4

Antifa and the Pathologies of Powerlessness

Inevitably, a lot of what I talk about in this book features on online left spaces. And a lot of leftists have insulated their minds against any critique of how toxic such spaces can be by telling themselves that online doesn't really matter. *If you're bothered by the way the left acts online, just spend less time on social media. Go for a run and get some fresh air.*

There are multiple reasons why this response is inadequate. For one thing, no one really believes it—at least not in any consistent way. Here's a simple example: A leftist man is harassing a leftist woman online. Maybe he keeps sending her pictures of his dick. She asks him to stop more than once and he ignores her. Let's say they're both in the same DSA chapter. Does anyone think for a second that the response of their comrades either would or should be to ignore the man's behavior and tell the woman to stop getting so upset about what goes on in an unimportant sphere like online? (*Spend less time on social media. Go for a run!*) For another, while it's true that face-to-face organizing is an indispensable and in many respects irreplaceable tool, it's absurd to talk in 2020 as if online wasn't a sphere in which a *massive* amount of political interaction and political persuasion (and, yes, even quite a bit of organizing) takes place.

A third reason why this is an inadequate response is that while these problems are often most glaringly obvious in online spaces, the underlying pathologies are *also* exhibited by segments of the offline left. Let's talk, for example, about "antifa."

I've been around left-wing circles long enough that the first time I heard that word was in the late 1990s. Oddly, a lot of right-wingers (and more than a few centrists) seem to be convinced that this is (a) the name of an organization that (b) formed sometime after Donald Trump became president and (c) represents a grave threat to public order and possibly national security. All of this would be hilarious if not for the troubling possibility that the Trump Administration might weaponize these fears to justify neo-McCarthyite state repression.

As a matter of fact, the abbreviation of "anti-fascist" to "antifa" originated in German leftist groups operating decades before I first heard the term. It names not an organization but a movement and a set of tactics. Roughly, "antifa" are protestors (often wearing masks and taking other precautions against the police) who aggressively confront neo-Nazis, Klansmen, Proud Boys, and similar fascist or fascist-like organizations. Sometimes these confrontations are violent, although very often they are not.

A lot of people on the far left are drawn to "antifa" activism for at least three reasons—two entirely reasonable, one much less so. First, pretty much the entire history of fascist organizations, ranging from Mussolini's "blackshirts" and Hitler's "brownshirts" to the kind of pissant outfit with 20 members that probably ended up calling itself the "Confederated Knights of the Invisible Empire of the Ku Klux Klan" because all the other variations on the Klan's name had already been taken by rival splinter groups, shows that such groups are prone to violence from their earliest stages and that "communists" are likely to be among the very first targets of that violence. Second, in my experience radical leftists are far less likely than other Americans (or at least other white Americans) to trust the police to protect them rather than to look for any excuse to beat up or arrest *them* and leave the fascists alone. And you know what? Fair enough on both points.

The third part of the equation, though, is that far too many American socialists get most of their understanding of radical politics not from any sort of analysis of what's going on around them in the here and now but from reading the works of long-dead revolutionaries. If you've spent enough time poring over Leon Trotsky's writings about the rise of fascism in Germany and what should have been done by German Socialists and Communists to defeat the brownshirts before they could seize power, it can be easy to forget that the 18 members of the Confederated Knights of the Invisible Empire of the Ku Klux Klan rallying on the courthouse steps (two of the Knights couldn't make it to the rally), surrounded by three hundred policemen and fifteen hundred counter-protestors, don't actually represent a remotely comparable threat to anyone in 2020. Their members may well commit hate crimes, but even if every single KKK and neo-Nazi-type organization in the United States dissolved itself tomorrow, the statistical shift in the overall hate crime rate probably wouldn't be that noticeable.

In Europe in the 20s and 30s, a major threat to organized labor came from gangs of fascist streetfighters busting up union halls and attacking organizers in back alleys. In the contemporary United States, this doesn't happen. The fascists simply don't have the numbers or the support, and big business by and large has nothing to gain from allying itself with such strange and distasteful fringe organizations. When employers need the services of violent strikebreakers, they either use the regular police or respectable private security firms. Besides, according to the US Bureau of Labor Statistics there were all of 20 "major work stoppages" in 2019 (as opposed to hundreds every year throughout the late 40s and the 50s, 60s, and 70s), so corporate America's current need for thugs of any kind to crack the heads of striking workers is pretty minimal. The current rate of private-sector unionization in the United States is an abysmal 6.4 percent—even though poll after poll shows that most workers would love to join a union if they had the chance. The long decline of the labor movement over the course of the last several decades (which has in turn led to wages-adjusted-for-inflation stagnating even as productivity has skyrocketed) has nothing to do with fascist violence. Actually, relevant factors range from unions themselves pursuing ineffective strategies to politicians of both parties embracing trade pacts that make it easy for employers to threaten to shut down operations and move to countries with more compliant workforces to America having some of the most worker-unfriendly labor laws in the developed world. (It's legal for companies to hire permanent replacements for striking workers, for example, and illegal for one group of workers to go out on a "sympathy strike" to support the efforts of another.) Similarly, the neo-Nazis and KKK and the rest—what antifa activists sometimes call "the fash"—don't rate on a list of the Top 100 threats to racial minorities, gay and trans people, and other traditional victims of fascist violence. The racial wealth gap, for example, has been widening in recent decades—not because of fascists burning down black businesses or re-enacting horrors like the race riot that destroyed Tulsa's "Black Wall Street" in 1921, but because the two main interrelated drivers of black upward mobility in the twentieth century (labor unions and the growth of public sector employment) have been systematically undermined. Even when it comes to violent confrontations on street corners, the white racists most likely to kill unarmed black men wear police uniforms, not Klan robes. This too has a lot to do with the kind of large-scale structural trends that can't be countered by punching anyone in the face—in this case the increasing militarization of police forces that have gobbled up more and more power over ordinary citizens as a result of the never-ending 'Wars' on Drugs and Terror. All of this is worth stressing, not just because an excessive focus on 'the fash' in America in 2019 can all too quickly devolve into an embarrassing form of political LARP-ing (Live Action Role-Playing) but because viewing a real but comparatively minor threat in apocalyptic terms can lead to tactical decisions that are severely counterproductive in terms of vastly more important strategic priorities.

Again: Fascist movements—even quite peripheral ones— really are prone to violence. Counting on the police to side with the fascists' victims really can be a risky proposition. And a group like the Proud Boys is both less marginal than fascist grouplets of the "Confederated Knights" variety and somewhat bolder about starting fights in the middle of the street in the middle of the day. I'm not prepared to say that there's no legitimate role to be played by antifa or something like it. One of the left-wing public intellectuals I admire most, Dr Cornel West, has said that antifa activists saved his life during the infamous "Unite the Right" rally in Charlotesville, and I believe him. A better iteration of antifa, though, wouldn't be an anarchistically loose cluster of individuals and small groups pursuing similar goals. It would be tightly organized and disciplined and (crucially) it would strictly prohibit the use of violence when the other side didn't throw the first punch—if only because this more strategically useful version of antifa would know that any policy other than this one would play into the hands of a media determined to demonize them and be used as an excuse for police repression.

The gap separating this vision of antifa from the way that far too much of this activism currently happens, with individuals or small "affinity groups" making decisions based on what feels right in the moment rather than carrying out any sort of well-thought-out strategy, was vividly demonstrated by the 2019 assault of Andy Ngo by antifa activists.

Ngo is a right-wing propagandist with very little interest in honest journalism. One small example: He wrote an article for the *Wall Street Journal* called "A Visit to Islamic England" in which he assumed that "Alcohol-Free Zone" signs in Muslim neighborhoods were a sign of creeping Sharia Law rather than just a sign that British law generally restricts public drinking. If he'd bothered visiting some otherwise similar non-Muslim neighborhoods, he'd have seen the same signs there.

After the assault, some of my leftist friends were intent on arguing that this sort of nonsense made Ngo *not a journalist*, but I'd argue that focusing on that semantic issue is dangerously misguided. Think about WikiLeaks, which has published revelations about the crimes of the American Empire in Iraq and elsewhere and has in return been subject to all sorts of legal and extra-legal harassment by the United States and its allies. As I write this, WikiLeaks founder Julian Assange is facing extradition to the United States for, among other charges, "soliciting and publishing classified information"—even though he isn't even a citizen of the country whose government classified that information. Pretty much everyone to the left of Chuck Schumer has rightly argued that this poses a grave threat to global press freedom, even though (a) there's at least some reason to think Julian Assange may actually be a terrible person—he hasn't gone on trial for this crime, but he's been accused of rape—and (b) Assange-hating Republicans and centrist Democrats love to argue that what WikiLeaks does doesn't count as "journalism" because they have, at least in some cases, just dumped uncurated information onto the internet.

Or think about Glenn Greenwald. He was working as a lawyer when he became increasingly alarmed by the warmongering and civil liberties violations of the Bush Administration. This led him to write a book and start a personal blog and then to write for *Salon*, *The Guardian*, and now *The Intercept*. During Greenwald's time at *The Guardian*, a brave National Security Agency (NSA) contractor named Edward Snowden sought him out and leaked information to him about the NSA's illegal mass surveillance activities (which then-Director of National Intelligence James Clapper had lied through his teeth about to Congress). More recently, Greenwald and his associates have been the recipients of leaks about the politically motivated prosecution of former Brazilian president Lula da Silva. At this point, Greenwald is one of the most prominent (and, from my perspective, one of the most admirable) investigative journalists in the world.

On the other hand, his critics can point out, Greenwald has no special training as a journalist. His BA is in philosophy. (As a philosophy instructor, I take this as a point of pride for my profession—just as I take the sloppy arguments of philosophy major Sam Harris as a point of professional shame. I don't always agree with Greenwald, but I do always admire his clear and precise style of argumentation.) His only postgraduate degree is a JD.

Nor was Greenwald's reporting of the Snowden revelations the product of any sort of gumshoe reporting. Snowden trusted him with the leaks because he knew from Greenwald's opinion writing that Greenwald was a fiercely principled critic of the sort of abuses that Snowden wanted to expose. If Greenwald had been subject to an Assange-style extradition effort, or if he'd been beaten up by some Brazilian fascists angry at his exposure of wrongdoing in their country, it's all too easy to imagine how those who might want to minimize the importance of what had happened could say, "Well, he's not a *real* journalist..."

Or, just to be all crass and selfish about this, think about *me*. I'm a columnist for *Jacobin* magazine. If you want to double-check any of the factual claims I make in my column, I'm sure you can easily reconstruct my Google searches. *Jacobin* editor Bhaskar Sunkara asked me to start writing for him because he liked my book about arguments. Like Greenwald (or Julian Assange, who studied mathematics, physics, and computer programming, but never graduated from college), I have no special training as a journalist. Unlike the two of them, I've never exposed any scandalous government or private-sector secrets and I'm not likely to do so. All the same, I hope that if someone beat me up because they didn't like something I'd written in *Jacobin*, everyone would be horrified by that and that one of the reasons they'd be horrified is that they'd be concerned about the chilling effect on left-wing media. In other words, to the extent that we care enough about press freedom to not only oppose *state* repression but to have a social norm against beating people up for what they write in the press, I'd like to think I'm protected by that norm. And I certainly hope that no one would feel the need to *first* have a discussion about whether what I'd written in that week's *Jacobin* article was entirely fair to its targets or whether I qualified as a "real" journalist before *then* deciding that I was covered by the no-beating-up-journalists taboo.

If Andy Ngo was being considered for a journalism award, I'd be against it because he's a silly hack. In *that* context, I might even start using phrases like "not a real journalist." But none of that should have anything to do with the norm against beating people up because we don't like the content of what they write.

A more plausible-sounding reason to think the assault on Ngo might fall under a legitimate exception to this norm is that he's been alleged to have "provided a kill list to Atomwaffen." This sounds like it complicates the issue...until you start to dig into the details of what exactly the accusation amounts to in practice.

The source of the "Atomwaffen kill list" allegation was a *Quillette* article by Eoin Lenihan entitled, "It's Not Your Imagination: The Journalists Writing About Antifa are Often Their Cheerleaders." The thesis of the article was absurd. (In real life, most media coverage of antifa is relentlessly unsympathetic to the point of equating them with the actual fascists.) The supporting evidence was worse than shoddy. Lenihan took journalists who cover antifa *following antifa accounts on Twitter* as a sign of ideological sympathy. Since so much of what I do, in my *Jacobin* articles and in my Debunk segments on *The Michael Brooks Show*, is about taking apart bad arguments made by right-wing writers, I follow a whole rogues gallery of conservative figures on Twitter. Applying Lenihan's logic, I must be a "cheerleader" for the lot of them.

It's not clear what Andy Ngo's level of involvement was with the article. He has a photo credit for the accompanying picture of masked protestors, and he's mentioned once or twice in the body of the piece, but there's no indication that he helped write it or that he was even an important research source. But let's assume for the sake of argument that he was actually an unacknowledged co-author.

The Atomwaffen Division is a neo-Nazi organization. Several of its members are in prison or facing charges for ideologically motivated violence. And they put out a menacing video in which they name-checked the same journalists in the same order that they'd appeared in Lenihan's article. This may or may not be a coincidence. At any rate I find it plausible that the fascists read and liked Lenihan's (or for the sake of argument Lenihan's and Ngo's) hacky article. Happily, as the months have passed, as far as I know no one has attempted to commit violence against anyone mentioned in the video. This isn't to say that those mentioned there have nothing to worry about or that they don't have every reason to be concerned. But even if Ngo *had* helped write Lehinan's piece—hell, even if he'd been the sole author—it would still be completely wrong to describe writing an article whose subjects were later threatened by fascists as "providing a kill list" to those fascists. *At best*, this is a particularly egregious example of an all-too-common form of sloppy reasoning identified by Adolph Reed in his indispensable book *Class Notes*—"has a similar effect as = might as well be = is." If I write an article for *Jacobin* in which I mention the accusation that Pacific Gas & Electric started wildfires in California by not securing their powerlines as part of my case for nationalizing the company, and some reader who admires the tactics of Alexander Berkman-era anarchists (look it up) does something stupid to a PG&E executive, I haven't provided this person with a kill list—and if you say I have, then you aren't making the basic distinction we're all making when we say that the core activities we normally think are protected by the laws (and associated social taboos) protecting press freedom should in fact be protected no matter what anyone does with what they *see* in the press.

Many of the details regarding what happened to Ngo are disputed. At least some claims seemed fanciful even at the time. (The Portland Police Department initially helped to spread rumors that a milkshake thrown at Ngo contained "liquid concrete" or "quick-drying cement" or some other nonsense that probably wouldn't be physically possible to mix with a milkshake in a paper cup.) Here's how a writer I *do* like and trust, *Current Affairs* editor Nathan Robinson, summarized what happened:

> On June 29th, the far right "Proud Boys" group, which is known for both making threats of violence and initiating street fights, staged a demonstration in Portland, Oregon. Because it is Portland, they were outnumbered by left-wing counter-demonstrators, including Antifa. Andy Ngo attended to cover the counter-demonstration. According to Ngo, as soon as he arrived, he was set upon by Antifa members who threw multiple milkshakes on him, then later began to pummel him and throw stones and eggs at him. A video of the event shows a milkshake-drenched Ngo being attacked and sprayed with silly string, pursued as he leaves the protest. Ngo went to the emergency room where he was diagnosed with a brain hemorrhage. Conservatives quickly rallied to support Ngo, raising nearly $200,000 on GoFundMe.

I'd recommend the rest of Robinson's article, entitled "Discipline, Strategy, and Morality," for a typically clear and thoughtful exploration of the issues raised by the attack. Robinson is another of those writers whose early academic training in philosophy seems to have paid off. Natalie Wynn, who I'll be discussing later in the book, is a third.

Concurring with Robinson, I thought at the time—and still

think—that no matter how inaccurate and inflammatory Ngo's reporting on antifa may have been, hospitalizing a noncombatant was both morally and strategically indefensible. (It's hard to imagine a faster way of getting a whole lot of people who could have gone either way to become disgusted with you and buy into a false equivalency between antifa and the fascists.) I was even more disturbed when I started noticing that some of my friends and comrades who disagreed with me about the Ngo incident didn't seem to be thinking about the "strategically" part at all.

I could sympathize with the resentment felt by my fellow radical leftists at being lectured on morality by centrists who've supported foreign wars, domestic mass incarceration, and other policies that have destroyed untold millions of lives. (I don't think that these critics having supported worse makes "just one brain hemorrhage" acceptable—that would be the *tu qoque* fallacy, or roughly "whataboutism"—but I do get why people find that kind of breathtaking hypocrisy grating.) My primary interest here is in the strategic dimension of the issue. Again, I find the terminology of decision theory useful. What utility do you hope to gain by beating up a journalist (or by going on Twitter and making excuses for beating up journalists)? How does this stack up against the obvious disutility of making antifa look like deranged thugs? What are the chances that any of this is going to have good results for the left?

In a few cases, people feeling defensive about the moral part of the question told me, *Hey, this is probably the best thing that could have happened for Ngo's career* in about the same spirit as people feeling defensive about Twitter pile-ons might say, *Whatever, all these people's careers are fine, no one is really canceled.*

In both cases, a few seconds of thought should be enough to show that these would be premises in excellent strategic arguments *against* the behaviors in question. If beating up a right-wing crank is actually good for his career, isn't that an excellent reason (above and beyond any purely moral considerations) *not* to do it? (I've heard some viewers of the Ngo assault video argue that he was intentionally baiting the antifa activists into attacking him. Let's assume for the sake of argument that this is correct. Doesn't it reinforce the point that smarter and better-disciplined antifa activists wouldn't have taken the bait?) If *no one is really canceled*—if, in other words, emotionally toxic behavior that makes potentially persuadable people want to run in the opposite direction from us doesn't even succeed in inconveniencing its targets—then what the hell is the point?

Heresy-hunting frenzies have taken place within political and religious factions that have actually held state power. The Salem Witch Trials and Mao's "Cultural Revolution" are obvious examples. A variety of factors best explained by psychologists, sociologists, anthropologists, and cognitive scientists are clearly at work in inspiring and sustaining such frenzies. (One small factor relevant to current online iterations of this phenomenon which Jon Ronson discusses at the end of his book *So You've Been Publicly Shamed* is that social media sites that let people see how many people have 'liked' their comments psychologically disincentivize users from questioning narratives popular in their groups. You get instant reinforcement for signaling loyalty to your tribe and its preferred view of things.) That said, the specific way in which contemporary leftists tend to tear each other apart over the pettiest possible nonsense has a lot to do with the fact that it's been a long, long time since we got anywhere close to the levers of real-world political power. One thing that *all* of the flaws of the contemporary left I discuss in this book have in common is that they're symptoms of what I've come to think of as *the pathologies of powerlessness*.

The labor movement has been in decline for several decades. Politicians Bernie Sanders in the US and Jeremy Corbyn in the UK spent most of their careers as extremely marginal figures. In terms of horizons more radical than the election platforms of Sanders and Corbyn, the collapse of deeply flawed and authoritarian experiments in creating non-capitalist economies in countries like the USSR led to a global consensus that, in the immortal words of the hideous Margaret Thatcher, "There is no alternative" to the way the world is presently organized.

The political atmosphere has started to change so quickly that it's hard to remember just how bad things were just a few years ago. As a leftist in the age of TINA (There Is No Alternative), you either rooted for corporate centrists like Bill Clinton and Barack Obama or you sat on the political sidelines rereading the Collected Works of Marx and Engels. Or you convinced yourself that the most small-scale forms of local activism would someday somehow amount to something.

In effect, anyone with a worldview to the left of liberalism was faced with a choice between just becoming a liberal or growing to see politics as a kind of moral performance. If you'd read your Chomsky and you paid attention to the news and you knew that both of the Democratic presidents in your lifetime had signed trade deals that undercut the bargaining power of once-mighty industrial unions and had bombed a whole lot of civilians in third-world countries, you might end up doing things like voting for third party candidates who the majority of Americans had literally never heard of in order to vent your displeasure. And why not? It helped preserve your sense of being part of some kind of opposition to all the infuriating things you read about in the newspaper, and it's not like there were enough people like you out there to tip the election to the Republicans in any case.

As with the *no one is really canceled* objection to left critiques of cancel culture, the underlying posture here is *hey, why are you picking on us powerless leftists, just let us have our impotent gesture of protest*. The thought that it might be possible to do better and actually have some kind of impact on real politics doesn't even arise.

Since I try to be a materialist—i.e. to understand the myriad ways in which, as Karl Marx put it in *The Eighteenth Brumaire of Louis Napoleon*, "men make their own history...but they do not make as they please, under circumstances of their own making"—I should acknowledge that up until relatively recently the central premise of this defense wasn't entirely wrong. There *weren't* a lot of openings for the left to meaningfully advance its goals in the real world.

Under those circumstances, it's understandable that a lot of radicals devoted a lot of their time to left-wing faction fights—often ones waged over fairly minor disagreements. If you can't change the big world outside the windows of the university lecture hall where your 50-member socialist organization holds its meetings, you can at least have the satisfaction of taking over the organization and bending *it* to your will. (That's a lot of what seems to have been going on in Tucker Carlson's clips of the DSA Convention. The real world is full of landlords and business-owners who won't do basic things to come into compliance with the decades-old Americans with Disabilities Act because no one with the energy and the financial resources to do so has made a plausible threat to sue them yet. Changing that reality is immensely difficult. But if you can at least get the DSA Convention to accommodate every last demand you dream up you can tell yourself that you're racking up victories *somewhere* for the rights of the disabled.) You can't stop plutocrats and war criminals from ruining the world. You can't even vent your displeasure at them in any forum where they're likely to notice. You *can* take other leftists to task for all the ways in which you judge them to be subtly wrong.

The big picture is finally starting to change. In 2008, as the Marxist economist Richard Wolff notes in his excellent book *Democracy at Work: The Alternative to Capitalism*, the taboo against nationalizing anything was so strong that when the federal government bailed out our "too big to fail" financial institutions, it mostly did so by buying up *non-voting* shares. The debate about the bailout pitted the Congressional majority of "responsible serious people" who supported it against a few dissident libertarian-leaning Republicans who wanted to let it all crash and then allow the invisible hand of the free market to pick up the pieces, and a few dissident populist Democrats who grumbled about socializing the losses of private companies but didn't have much of an alternative to offer. It's an indication of how much things have changed in the last 12 years, between Occupy Wall Street, the two presidential campaigns of Bernie Sanders, and the rise of DSA from a glorified mailing list of several hundred names to an organization with several tens of thousands of active members and multiple members of Congress that it's impossible to imagine the same thing happening now without some loud voices being raised in favor of nationalizing the banks and running them in the public interest.

To be clear, we wouldn't *win* that battle even now. To do that, we'd probably need (a) massive majority support, (b) control of the elected branches of government, and (c) a militant, well-developed grassroots political infrastructure, *starting* with an overwhelmingly unionized workforce, that could back the play of this hypothetical socialist government with general strikes and unrest on the streets—but our position would have been part of the debate. That's progress.

In the first chapter of Bhaskar Sunkara's book *The Socialist Manifesto*, he imagines a transition to socialism involving publicly owned banks seeding investment capital to worker cooperatives (and existing businesses being reorganized as coops). We can already point to plenty of real-world examples of successful worker coops like Spain's Mondragon Corporation. All Sunkara had to do to arrive at a realistic and grounded vision of socialism was to imagine workers' control scaling up to dominate the private sector as a whole in combination with a more fully developed version of the kind of universal social programs we've already seen in the Nordic countries and elsewhere.

If the same book had been published 20 years ago, the only

reviews would have been factional takedowns in rival socialist publications. In 2019, Sunkara's book attracted a decent amount of attention in the mainstream press. He was interviewed by *The New Yorker* after the book came out, he discussed the finer points of his view of socialism with Michelle Goldberg of *The New York Times*, he debated his ideas with libertarian economist Gene Epstein at the Soho Forum, and so on.

Jacobin's Micah Uetricht captured some of the ways the political landscape has changed for the better in an essay entitled "The Beginning of the End of Capitalist Realism" that marked the 2-year anniversary of Mark Fisher's death.

> Capitalist realism, [Fisher] wrote in his book of the same name, is "the widespread acceptance that there is no alternative to capitalism." It's not an enthusiastic embrace of neoliberal capitalism—that embrace has long passed, if it ever existed. Rather, it's a widespread sense of resignation over the foregone conclusion that neoliberal capitalism is the only game in town...
>
> We can see capitalist realism beginning to break here in the United States, in the wild successes of Bernie Sanders and the explosion of the Democratic Socialists of America, in the warp-speed transformations of public consciousness around Medicare for All and free college for all and taxing the hell out of the rich.

The reversal of Bernie Sanders' fortunes over the course of the 2020 Democratic primaries is a depressing reminder that, even when it comes to the social democratic basics like Medicare for All, we're nowhere close to *winning* yet. Even so, the space of what's considered up for debate in mainstream politics has definitely shifted in our direction...which is why it's a shame that there are still so many leftists who seem bound and determined to destroy any hope of winning majority support for a transition to a humane and democratic post-capitalist future by failing to clearly differentiate the kind of socialism we want from the discredited and authoritarian "socialism" of economically sclerotic one-party states.

Let's talk about "tankies."

5

Tankies are Wreckers

The basic normative impulse behind socialist politics can be most simply summarized like this: *The division of society into a class of people who own businesses and a class of people with no realistic choice except to go to work for the first class, thus submitting to near-total control of all aspects of their lives for eight out of every 16 waking hours, five days a week, is deeply unjust. It's possible to organize society in a way that avoids this division. Let's organize the working class to make that happen.*

The first major attempt at creating a socialist society was the Russian Revolution in 1917. The original revolutionaries understood socialism as an *expansion* of democracy from the political sphere into the structure of workplaces. They thought the effect of their revolution was going to be to put the working class in charge of society. The question of "what went wrong" is immensely complicated, but part of the answer has to do with the fact that the Russian Empire before 1917 was still a mostly peasant society. The cities were islands of modern industrial capitalism, but the working class was a relatively small minority of the population. This meant that what would in America or a western European country have been a movement by and for the majority of society was in the Russian context the movement of a minority that (at best) existed in an uneasy alliance with the peasant majority even as it fought off foreign invaders and domestic counterrevolutionary armies. The "at best" broke down as the situation became more desperate. Armed detachments from the cities were sent to "requisition" grain from unwilling peasants to feed the urban workers and the soldiers of the Red Army. This had the entirely predictable consequence of giving the peasants very little incentive to produce anything, and this caused more severe food shortages and drove the Soviet government to crack down harder.

Another part of what went wrong is that the Bolshevik leaders were far too willing to give up basic democratic principles held dear by previous generations of socialists for the sake of defending the besieged revolution. As with many countries with armies marching back and forth across their territory, civil liberties like the right to a fair trial went out the window pretty much as soon as the shooting started.

Victor Serge, who was himself an active Bolshevik in those early years, put this point sharply in a 1938 exchange with his fellow revolutionary Leon Trotsky. Serge and Trotsky agreed that the Soviet Union had long since become a parody of the vision for which they'd originally fought but Trotsky was still in denial about how early the rot had set in.

The question which dominates today the whole discussion is, in substance, this: When and how did Bolshevism begin to degenerate?

When and how did it begin to employ towards the toiling masses, whose energy and highest consciousness it expressed, non-socialist methods which must be condemned because they ended by assuring the victory of the bureaucracy over the proletariat?

This question posed, it can be seen that the first symptoms of the evil date far back. In 1920, the Menshevik social-democrats were falsely accused, in a communiqué of the Cheka, of intelligence with the enemy, of sabotage, *etc.* This communiqué, monstrously false, served to outlaw them. In the same year, the anarchists were arrested throughout Russia, after a formal promise to legalize the movement and after the treaty of peace signed with Makhno had been deliberately torn up by the Central Committee which no longer needed the Black Army. The revolutionary correctness of the totality of a policy cannot justify, in my eyes, these baneful practices. And the facts that I cite are unfortunately far from being the only ones.

Let us go back still further. Has not the moment come to declare that the day of the glorious year of 1918 when the Central Committee of the party decided to permit the Extraordinary Commissions to apply the death penalty *on the basis of secret procedure, without hearing the accused who could not defend themselves*, is a black day? That day the Central Committee was in a position to restore or not restore an Inquisitional procedure forgotten by European civilization. In any case, it committed a mistake. It did not necessarily behoove a victorious socialist party to commit that mistake. The revolution could have defended itself better without that.

The moral problem with the practices Serge criticizes is too obvious to need to be spelled out. The strategic issue about the probability of various possible consequences of the Bolsheviks' decisions and their utility or disutility for achieving socialist goals require a bit more unpacking. The problem is that even if you're willing to sign off on such methods for the sake of achieving your goal of a classless society, the methods are flatly incompatible with the goal. You can't "temporarily" abandon the most basic civil liberties *and* extend democracy at the same time. When Soviet citizens started to see that being accused of counterrevolutionary sympathies was a death sentence, most of them learned not to express controversial political opinions of any kind. Mass popular participation in government or the economy—even to the extent that such participation was still allowed—was pretty quickly reduced to the status of a legal fiction. The end result of all this wasn't the originally desired end to a division of society into a class of workers and a class of owners in favor of some sort of radically democratic alternative but the substitution of a new division of society into a class of workers and a class of party bosses and state officials who essentially filled the role vacated by the old private capitalists. By the time the various opposition movements that arose within the party during the 1920s started to push to restore some measure of democracy, it was far too late. In the 1930s, men and women who'd devoted their lives to the revolution—both former oppositionists and unlucky Stalin loyalists who had randomly come under suspicion—were being executed or sent to prison camps on absurd charges ranging from being Nazi spies to being "wreckers" working to maliciously undermine the fulfillment of the state's economic goals. Even if later Soviet leaders were far less brutal, Stalin's reign of terror stands as an indictment of the Soviet system for the same reason that Caligula's reign of terror stands as an indictment of the Roman Empire. These systems created the possibility of Stalins and Caligulas by concentrating immense power at the top with no democratic accountability or constitutional restraints.

It's important to note that when right-wing anti-communists say that "every" attempt at replacing capitalism with socialism ends this way (with the implication being that any *future* attempt at bringing about socialist democracy will have the same authoritarian result), they're making a sloppy argument. The accurate thing to say is that exactly one attempt at replacing capitalism with a socialist democracy ended with authoritarianism. Subsequent transitions to communism in countries like China, Vietnam, and the Soviet satellite states in Eastern Europe weren't attempts to create socialist democracy. They were self-conscious attempts to recreate what existed in the Soviet Union initiated by Communist parties whose leaders were ideologically committed to that model.

We can (and should) both walk and chew bubblegum when it comes to our retrospective evaluation of these societies. Not everything we can learn from these experiments is negative. It's possible, for example, to criticize Cuba's regime for not having a free press or multi-party elections while also acknowledging their impressive strides in healthcare, education, and racial desegregation—not to mention sending doctors all around the world to help out in natural disasters, sending troops to help defeat Apartheid South Africa, and holding out against decades of US-backed terrorism and economic sanctions. Neither the accomplishments nor the authoritarianism need to be denied or minimized in a mature left analysis of Cuba's complicated reality.

Even East Germany had its positive aspects. Kristen Ghodsee examines evidence in her book *Why Women Had Better Sex Under Socialism* that sexual and romantic relationships in East Germany tended to be more egalitarian and better for women than those in West Germany because of the relatively more egalitarian spread of wealth and the existence of sweeping programs guaranteeing social rights to the basic goods of life. East German men couldn't compensate for having terrible personalities or being bad in bed by being rich and East German women didn't stay in bad relationships because they didn't have the financial resources to strike out on their own.

We don't need to reduce the whole experience of capital-C Communism to a cartoonish caricature entirely defined by bread lines and gulags in order to be critical of that system. But we *should* be critical of it, both because those regimes objectively deserve criticism and because failure to make a clear distinction between what existed in a society like East Germany and what we advocate now would be fatal to the prospects for winning majority support for socialism.

Workers in all of these states were well aware of the gap between the official fictions (the Eastern European regimes, for example, called themselves "People's Democracies") and their own near-total lack of control over the structures that governed their lives. This tension led to many strikes and uprisings in the Eastern Bloc throughout the late twentieth century. One of the most famous of these was the Hungarian Revolution of 1956. The Hungarians actually set up workers councils (just like Russian workers had in 1917) and tried to fulfill the original radically democratic aspirations of the Russian Revolution...until the experiment was crushed by a Soviet military intervention.

As far as I know the word "tankie" was first used as a slang term in British far left circles to describe those western leftists who supported Krushchev's decision to send Soviet tanks to crush the Hungarian Revolution and similar decisions by later Soviet leaders. Over the course of the decades since that revolution "tankie" has evolved into a catch-all term for western leftist defenders of communist one-party states.

One would think that the near-total collapse of what tankies called "actually existing socialism" near the end of the twentieth century would have put an end to all of that (especially since one of the reasons for the collapse of that system was the mass dissatisfaction of ordinary people who lived under those regimes). Oddly, though, there's been a noticeable resurgence of "tankie" attitudes, not only in online leftist spaces but even among a certain fringe of DSA members. This last development is especially hard to understand when you remember that the only reason the organization ever called itself the "Democratic" Socialists of America was to differentiate the sort of "socialism" that it advocates from Soviet-style authoritarianism. So what gives? Where are the contemporary "tankies" coming from?

Micah Uetricht has suggested that "there's a thrill that comes along with breaking the taboo established by McCarthyism." If communist regimes were misrepresented in Cold War propaganda, some western leftists have a simplistic but half-understandable drive to "bend the stick all the way in the other direction."

Another part of the answer is that a certain kind of leftist thinks like this: *Who am I to judge the mistakes of past revolutionaries, who often had to deal with desperate conditions that I can't possibly*

61

imagine, from the perspective of my café or podcast studio or DSA meeting in Brooklyn in the twenty-first century? Instead of trashing these past attempts at creating a better society, we should focus on defending their record against imperialist lies and propaganda.

I can sympathize with the impulse underlying this line of thought. One problem with it, though, is that it relies on multiple conflations of very different ideas. One such conflation has already been noted—that while it may be true that the Bolsheviks were trying to create a socialist democracy and inadvertently created Stalinism, Mao and Ho Chi Minh were already admirers of the model of centralized economic planning and an authoritarian one-party state *before* they took power. It wasn't something they fell into as a result of fraught decisions made under desperate circumstances. That's simply what they meant by "socialism."

Another point that people who think this way are missing is that an admirably humble and self-aware thought like, "If I were in the same situation, I may well have made all the same mistakes" is entirely compatible with, "I can recognize with hindsight that these policies *were* mistakes and indeed that they were ultimately fatal to the original goals of the revolution." You can sympathize with people navigating tragic historical circumstances and ending up on the wrong path while still keeping track of which path is which.

Tankies sometimes argue that revolutionaries like Fidel Castro *could only* have recreated the Soviet model, because allowing for political freedom and democratic elections would have allowed the CIA or other nefarious forces to take over their societies and restore capitalism. This has always struck me as more of a tankie article of faith than something backed up by good arguments. There's no doubt that leaders like Castro *believed* that this was the only way their revolutions could survive. But were they right? It's true enough that a US-backed coup took out the democratic socialist government of Salvador Allende in Chile. But it's also true the United States has successfully smashed plenty of authoritarian regimes. Having a police state doesn't give you any sort of magical immunity against coups or invasions or even mass protest movements a la Eastern Europe in 1989. It does, however, rule out the possibility that you'll end up with anything resembling "socialism" in the original sense of the word.

And eagerness to excuse undemocratic regimes that have called themselves "socialist" is almost perversely counterproductive in the current situation. It's one thing to hope to sell tens of millions of ordinary people on the goal of extending democracy from politics to economics. It's quite another to hope to sell them on the idea that the Soviet model of "socialism" might be about the best that can be hoped for and they should thus be prepared to give up the democratic rights they already have. As my friend and frequent collaborator Matt McManus put it in a discussion of this book, the optics of online leftists getting into pedantic arguments about exactly how many Chinese peasants starved to death in the Great Leap Forward could hardly be worse for anyone who cares about popularizing the socialist critique of the status quo.

Even if we have a nuanced view of what was good and bad about the "actually existing socialisms" of the twentieth century — acknowledging that it wasn't *all* gulags and breadlines — we need to acknowledge that the gulags and breadlines were a big part of the story. Even in the 70s and 80s when the Soviet Union and its satellites had undergone decades of reform and liberalization, they were deeply authoritarian societies in which elections were *pro forma* shams, workers had even less control over their work lives than western workers (who could at least legally organize independent trade unions), and the routine disconnects between consumer needs and the actual contents of grocery store shelves were a constant source of frustration for ordinary people.

Right-wing anti-communists may have told plenty of lies

about the Soviet Union over the decades, but even if they hadn't, the reality of Soviet life would have functioned as a fairly potent source of anti-communist propaganda all by itself. By the end of the Cold War, the Soviet leaders themselves had realized their system wasn't working. Otherwise, the bureaucracy never would have gone along with Gorbachev's reforms. And even in those capitalist democracies that *did* have large communist parties that played a serious role in their politics—e.g., Italy and France—very few people had any desire to emulate the Soviet model.

The turning point came when Soviet tanks rolled into Prague in 1968 to crush an experiment in liberalization that Czechoslovak leader Alexander Dubček called "socialism with a human face" and all but the most hardcore Moscow loyalists balked at once again being asked to defend the indefensible. After that, the PFC in France and the PCI in Spain, like several smaller communist parties, increasingly moved in the direction of an approach called "Eurocommunism" or "democratic communism." This meant that (a) they'd drifted away from uncritically defending the Soviet Union and (b) they became increasingly interested in pursuing a road to socialism from *within* their countries' democratic institutions.

In countries like the UK or (especially) the United States, where there had never been communist parties on the same scale as France or Italy in the first place, the idea that "communism" of any sort could be divorced from grim Soviet realities was foreign to most people. The UK at least had the Labour Party, whose large and powerful left wing stayed socialist even as its leadership drifted to the right, but to most Americans throughout the twentieth century, "socialist," "communist," and "Soviet" were more or less synonymous. Outside of the tiny state of Vermont, where one particularly skillful "democratic socialist" politician managed to get himself elected to Congress just as the Cold War was ending, no one who trafficked in *any* of these labels was going anywhere in mainstream politics.

Thirty years after the fall of the USSR, so-called "actually existing socialism" has receded far enough into the historical rearview mirror that all of this has finally started to change. This is a huge opportunity for the left to advance a humane and democratic vision of a post-capitalist society. I can't imagine a more maddeningly counterproductive response to that historic opportunity than insisting that *the Soviet Union was good actually* and re-blurring the distinction between the "socialism" of militarized one-party states and the better world that might finally be within our reach.

6

Neo-Anarchy in the UK (and in the United States)

Tankie-ism is one possible symptom of the pathologies of powerlessness discussed earlier in the book. Being distant from the levers of real power in their own societies, some leftists can't resist the temptation to live vicariously through over-identification with left (or "left") governments elsewhere in the world. An equal and opposite symptom of the same problem is what Mark Fisher called "neo-anarchism" in the essay I referred to earlier in the book—"Exiting the Vampire Castle."

"Anarchism" is a word that has historically meant a lot of different things. Some "anarchists" are frankly right-wing. Given the (relative) popularity of libertarianism in the contemporary United States, "anarcho-capitalists" aren't as vanishingly rare in this country as they are elsewhere.

A character in Kim Stanley Robinson's novel *Green Mars* quipped that those libertarians who say they want a "minimal state" are just "anarchists who want police protection from their slaves." To extend and possibly ruin Robinson's joke, an anarcho-capitalist is a libertarian who is consistent enough about his objections to taxation to be willing to make bosses in need of billy-club wielding strikebreakers rely on *private* security.

Historically, though, most people who've called themselves "anarchists" haven't been apologists for the economic status quo. Instead, their objections to the state flow from a generalized suspicion of hierarchical systems in both politics and economics. I think there's much to admire in this attitude, and in at least some of the things that anarchists have historically accomplished. For example, the anarchist-led IWW (Industrial Workers of the World) was one of the most important and effective labor unions in the United States in the early decades of the twentieth century. Anarchist militias played an important role in the struggle against fascism in Spain in the 1930s and the anarchist ideas of Murray Bookchin played a role in influencing the radical Kurdish movement in Rajova that engaged in a similarly heroic stand against ISIS in this century.

I'm not an anarchist for at least two reasons. First—and here I part ways even with completely orthodox Marxists who believe that the state will eventually "wither away"—I'm skeptical that even the most advanced socialist society could ever completely do without institutions like courts of law and even (humane, minimalistic, and rehabilitation-oriented) prisons. Imagine that we live in a materially abundant high-tech socialist utopia in the twenty-third century. Poverty and the crimes associated with poverty have long since become a thing of the past. The economic reorganization of society has left no room for organized crime to continue to exist. Even in this happy thought experiment, do we really think it's likely that interpersonal conflicts will literally *never* result in violence? That frustrated desire will never ever under any circumstances result in even a single rape anywhere in the world? And if we don't think that, then how do we imagine that a society without prisons punish these crimes? I hope the answer wouldn't be lynch mob justice, but if not, that strongly suggests the presence of institutions of involuntary confinement and some sort of court system. Perhaps, depending on how you understand the concept of a "state," you could argue that sufficiently localized and disconnected legal institutions wouldn't add up to a "state." If so, I'd worry that such a system wouldn't be centralized enough to have the kind of uniform protections of the rights of defendants that I value as a democratic socialist. You need a fair amount of centralization, for example, to get a change of venue if you're put on trial in a town where everyone hates you.

Perhaps all this just speaks to my lack of imagination. If so, I'll simply register as a data point for my readers' consideration that over the course of my decades of involvement with the left I've never met an anarchist who seemed to have well-worked-out answers to these questions. Perhaps I just haven't talked to the right anarchists. But whatever you make of that issue, a second problem with anarchism—or at least with what a lot of people who call themselves anarchists seem to mean by that term—is that even those anarchists whose political goals substantially overlap with mine often act as if anarchist principles would be violated by contesting elections with the goal of using the power of the state to advance those goals.

...and that brings us to Mark Fisher. Here's what he said about "neo-anarchism" in the British context in "Exiting the Vampire Castle":

> By neo-anarchists I definitely do not mean anarchists or syndicalists involved in actual workplace organisation, such as the Solidarity Federation. I mean, rather, those who identify as anarchists but whose involvement in politics extends little beyond student protests and occupations, and commenting on Twitter. Like the denizens of the Vampires' Castle, neo-anarchists usually come from a petit-bourgeois background, if not from somewhere even more class-privileged.
>
> They are also overwhelmingly young: in their twenties or at most their early thirties, and what informs the neo-anarchist position is a narrow historical horizon. Neo-anarchists have experienced nothing but capitalist realism. By the time the neo-anarchists had come to political consciousness— and many of them have come to political consciousness remarkably recently, given the level of bullish swagger they sometimes display—the Labour Party had become a Blairite shell, implementing neo-liberalism with a small dose of social justice on the side. But the problem with neo-anarchism is that it unthinkingly reflects this historical moment rather than

offering any escape from it. It forgets, or perhaps is genuinely unaware of, the Labour Party's role in nationalising major industries and utilities or founding the National Health Service. Neo-anarchists will assert that "parliamentary politics never changed anything", or the "Labour Party was always useless" while attending protests about the NHS, or retweeting complaints about the dismantling of what remains of the welfare state. There's a strange implicit rule here: it's OK to protest against what parliament has done, but it's not alright to enter into parliament or the mass media to attempt to engineer change from there. Mainstream media is to be disdained, but BBC Question Time is to be watched and moaned about on Twitter. Purism shades into fatalism; better not to be in any way tainted by the corruption of the mainstream, better to uselessly "resist" than to risk getting your hands dirty.

Fisher is obviously describing a historically specific context. While most of the rest of the essay is if anything disturbingly evergreen, some of the details of the political landscape he's commenting on have changed in some ways since 2013. In some ways, in fact, they've changed in just the ways that Fisher hoped they would. The take-over of the Labour Party by a left-wing movement led by Jeremy Corbyn was one of the most important victories for the socialist left in the developed world in a long, long time. (Needless to say, this makes the subsequent electoral defeat of the Corbynized Labour Party a devastating blow. That's one of the disadvantages of getting your hands dirty in real politics—when you let yourself get emotionally invested in the ups and downs of the day-to-day political struggle, you open yourself up to getting your heart broken. As I write this, the future political direction of the Labour Party is deeply uncertain.) Abstracting from these particular details, though, anyone who's been around a certain kind of DSA activist should recognize the impulses that Fisher is critiquing—and should recognize that these problems are hardly unique to those leftists who "call themselves anarchists."

It should go without saying that these things come in degrees. Lots of people who display neo-anarchist tendencies in many contexts were sufficiently swept up in the general enthusiasm for Bernie Sanders during the brief and glorious moment in early 2020 when it looked like he would be the Democratic nominee to knock on doors and donate money to the campaign. (Similarly, lots of people who display tankie tendencies will admit if pressed on the point that they would hope that the sort of socialism they help to bring about in this country would indeed include a broad array of democratic and civil rights.) "Tankie" and "neo-anarchist" are *types*. There are undeniably some leftists who are seemingly perfect representations of these types, but there are many more who embody a complicated mixture of useful and counterproductive political impulses.

That said, there are many examples of not only individual comrades but e.g. entire DSA branches whose activity is badly warped by neo-anarchist tendencies. I think that the brake light clinics discussed in the first chapter of this book can constitute a clever and useful community outreach tactic—*if* they're properly seen as a very small cog in a larger machine of socialist political activity that *centers* on far more strategically important matters like canvassing for Medicare for All and trying to elect left-wing politicians to office. Similarly, I'm all in favor of inviting comrades to go out to the bar after a meeting to have a few drinks and chat in a more informal way than you can in a public event. But I was perturbed, as Bernie Sanders' second run for president heated up in late 2019, to see that there were DSA chapters which were keeping up their brake light clinics and regularly scheduling "Socializing with Socialists" bar nights but that didn't seem to be doing a damn thing to elect the most pro-worker candidate to ever have a serious shot at the American

Presidency.

If you're socializing with other members of the organization and doing good works to bring visibility to that organization, and that's *all* you and your comrades are doing, you're a social club, not a socialist organization in the business of trying to change the world. And if you're organizing protests (i.e. "resisting") but not running candidates or organizing labor unions or doing much of anything else to build real-world power, then there's a good chance that you see politics as a symbolic performance of your personal opposition to injustice rather than as a serious effort to create a more just world. Finally, if what you take to matter most is the righteous opposition to the depravities of the world that you're carrying around in your individual soul, it's only natural that you'll end up spending a lot of time both trying to prove your personal virtue and examining the virtue of others.

...and that's where things get really ugly.

7

"No One Is Ever Really Canceled"

In the opening paragraphs of the Vampire Castle essay, Mark Fisher makes an observation that could have been made at literally any time in the ensuing 7 years:

> "Left-wing" Twitter can often be a miserable, dispiriting zone. Earlier this year, there were some high-profile twitterstorms, in which particular left-identifying figures were "called out" and condemned. What these figures had said was sometimes objectionable; but nevertheless, the way in which they were personally vilified and hounded left a horrible residue: the stench of bad conscience and witch-hunting moralism.

He goes on to give the examples of *Guardian* columnist Owen Jones and the comedian, actor, and left-wing commentator Russell Brand. If he'd written the essay in 2019 instead of 2013, he might have talked about Barbara Ehrenreich.

When the online mobs are getting worked up about a Bill Burr or a Dave Chappelle, there's at least a non-trivial possibility that the object of their outrage might actually have some flawed moral and political values—and I say that as someone who deeply admires both performers, and who thinks that poring through a standup special or any other work of art for moral and political flaws is usually a silly exercise that only serves to re-enforce the worst image of the left in the minds of the undecided. If a comic's on-stage rants about his relationship with his girlfriend involve an element of joke-y sexism, you can at least see where suspicions of underlying non-joke-y sexism are coming from. When the mob is yelling at someone like Barbara Ehrenreich, something much dumber is going on.

Ehrenreich has been part of the socialist movement, the women's movement, and the peace movement since the Vietnam era. She was a leader of the New American Movement (NAM), a group of left-wing intellectuals that later merged with Michael Harrington's Democratic Socialist Organizing Committee (DSOC) to become DSA. As she revealed in a recent interview with the leftist magazine *Dissent*, she was opposed to the merger at the time. Even though Harrington had been a dove on Vietnam, and Ehrenreich herself was a critic of the authoritarian Soviet model of socialism, one of her main concerns was that Harrington and DSOC were too inclined to a sort of "strongly anti-Communist socialism" that came too close to feeding into Cold War propaganda. The merger went through despite her reservations, and Ehrenreich served for a long time as an Honorary Co-Chair of the DSA. She's written a steady stream of books and essays for the last 50 years, often dealing with economic inequality, gender inequality, and America's brutal domination of the Global South, all from a "predictable-as-hell" humane and egalitarian perspective.

Fast forward to 2019. In a tweet about popular Japanese decluttering guru Marie Kondo, Ehrenreich mused out loud about what it might say that Kondo was this popular with American audiences despite the fact that she didn't speak English. Previous generations of mainstream television viewers wouldn't have been willing to read subtitles in exchange for that kind of content, and Ehrenreich tweeted that this was a sign that "America is in decline as a superpower."

It always feels strange to spell out in detail what you take to be the point of someone else's throwaway tweet, but here goes: *While America remains the world's dominant power, recent geopolitical shifts have complicated and somewhat undermined that dominance. This change has made itself felt in the cultural sphere, where we can see indications of the declining imperial arrogance of citizens of the United States. Americans once took it for granted that everyone in the world—certainly anyone with a claim on their attention—would learn their language but those expectations have begun to shift. Isn't that interesting?*

I suppose someone hearing Ehrenreich's name for the first time when the ensuing Twitter pile-on was in progress might be forgiven for thinking the point of her tweet was flag-waving "everyone should learn English" xenophobia, but anyone with any previous familiarity with the woman or her decades of writing and activism should know better. She's spent decades as a critic of the American Empire. Why on earth would she suddenly now think its decline was an unwelcome development?

As I watched hundreds of random Twitter users yelling at her, I kept thinking about something that happened when I was a teenager:

A couple who were friends with my parents had four dogs. Our family had two. One weekend the couple went out of town and left their dogs at our house. Ours met theirs, butts were sniffed, and the six of them did what any sufficiently large number of dogs will do. They formed into a pack and went romping around the house looking for things to bark at. When the pack found one of our cats, all six dogs—including the two who saw that cat every day without incident—started barking their heads off.

In this case, the group mind stupidity is even more unforgivable, since presumably the *first* dogs to start barking at Ehrenreich were the ones who *followed her on Twitter.* Anyone in that category would know that she'd been an anti-Empire activist since the presidency of Richard Nixon. Even so, the appearance on their timelines of a tweet that *could* be read differently if you forgot who tweeted it was enough to set them off, and that set others off, and by the time the whole thing was written up in outlets like *USA Today,* journalists who may or may not have even googled Ehrenreich's name at some point before penning their write-ups were casually referring to it as a "racist tweet."

Perhaps you can excuse the worst elements of the Very Online Left (and the lazy journalists who enable them by not doing their own research) for misdiagnosing Ehrenreich so badly. She comes from a previous generation of leftists and might be suspected of harboring all sorts of attitudes that were only recently discovered to be problematic. But no such suspicions could apply to Natalie Wynn and the Twitter mobs have been just as ludicrously uncharitable in interpreting her statements and just as relentless in hounding her for them.

Wynn, who's better known by the name of her YouTube channel ("Contrapoints"), is by far the most popular figure on what's sometimes called BreadTube (i.e. Left YouTube). Profiles of her have appeared in publications ranging from *Current Affairs* to *Vice* to *New York Magazine* and *The Atlantic*. She's a transwoman who often uses her videos to talk about trans rights, but she also has videos on topics ranging from capitalism to comedy to moral dilemmas about the acceptable use of violence.

She's a former philosophy graduate student, and it shows. Anyone who comes even close to finishing a PhD in philosophy has a truly absurd amount of training in taking arguments apart and putting them back together again. Those who *stay* in academia, though, rarely put these skills to use in the day-to-day political struggle going on outside their classroom windows. Some of this is because of disinterest or because that kind of work just naturally isn't for everyone but a lot of it is a result of structural features of academic philosophy. If you're one of the lucky few who lands one of the rapidly dwindling handful of tenure-track jobs left at increasingly corporate-ized, adjunct-ized universities, you'll be encouraged to spend a lot of your time writing. As Nathan Robinson points out in his article "Academics Cannot Evade Their Public Responsibilities," the only kind of writing that "counts" for the purposes of tenure and promotion is writing that's aimed at a handful of high-prestige academic journals that are only read by the people who try to publish there. (Other kinds of writing, like the book you're reading, would be regarded by a tenure committee as irrelevant at best and a waste of time at worst.) Meanwhile, the vast majority of academic philosophers have a very different set of problems. The typical philosopher is either driving around teaching Logic and Intro to Philosophy and Intro to Ethics classes as an adjunct at three different universities to string together some approximation of a full-time income (and buying health insurance from the Obamacare exchanges) or *at best* holding down a full-time renewable gig with health insurance but no job security—and the kind of teaching load not designed to leave time for writing of any kind.

Wynn managed to get enough philosophical training to have the skill set before she got off the academic treadmill and devoted herself to making videos for a popular (i.e. non-academic) audience. In her case, that audience is big enough for ad revenue and Patreon donations to keep her from needing to do anything else for a living. She combines a well-sharpened ability to dissect arguments with a dark sense of humor, a flair for atmosphere, and a way of narrating her videos that always manages to suggest that she's more interested in exploring the issues and having a little fun at the expense of the buffoons and the bigots than she is in preaching to her audience. Even when she's doing videos debunking the race mythology of lunatic white nationalists like Richard Spencer, she rarely gets angry. Her tone is closer to the one P.G. Wodehouse used to mock fascism in his novel *The Code of the Woosters*, in which Wodehouse's usually bumbling protagonist Bertie Wooster tells Roderick Spode, leader of the fictional Black Shorts, that, "it's about time some public-spirited person told you where you got off" and proceeds to deliver what Christopher Hitchens once called the greatest anti-fascist speech ever written in English.

The trouble with you, Spode, is that just because you have

succeeded in inducing a handful of half-wits to disfigure the London scene by going about in black shorts, you think you're someone. You hear them shouting "Heil, Spode!" and you imagine it is the Voice of the People. That is where you make your bloomer. What the Voice of the People is saying is: "Look at that frightful ass Spode swanking about in footer bags! Did you ever in your puff see such a perfect perisher?"

Back when Wynn was still on Twitter, you could find people ranging from ex-TERFs (Trans-Exclusionary Radical Feminists) to ex-Republicans to ex-Nazis telling her that she'd helped convince them that they were wrong. As such, you'd think that leftists who spend a lot of time on Twitter and YouTube would regard Natalie Wynn as their team's MVP.

...and, to be fair, that's probably the majority opinion. But a loud and depressingly significant minority have at this point bullied her off Twitter at least twice. The first of the two incidents I know of started with a thread in which Wynn expressed mild irritation with the now-common ritual of going around a room almost entirely made up of non-trans people and having everyone state their pronouns. She noted the uncomfortable irony that she can be "miss"-ed and "ma'am"-ed all night by the servers at a sports bar in North Carolina but in "progressive" "trans-friendly" spaces she feels awkwardly singled out as everyone's eyes go to her when it's her turn to publicly affirm her identity. Nowhere in the offending tweets did she say that her discomfort meant that no one should ever go around a room saying their pronouns again. Nor did she deny that some non-binary or non-passing trans people might have good reason to value this practice. Her crime—the entirety of her crime—was that she described her own mixed feelings.

The second time she was hounded off of Twitter had to do with Buck Angel, a trans icon of a previous generation who subscribes to a view called "transmedicalism." This, as I understand it, is the thesis that the only "real" trans people are the ones who suffer from medically diagnosable gender dysphoria and then medically transition. Angel has also been accused of behaving badly during an ugly divorce. The heart of the accusation is that he told journalists that another celebrity—who had been having an affair with Angel's wife—was a "cross-dresser." Since the celebrity in question came out as a transwoman many years later, Angel has been retroactively accused of outing this person *as trans*, although he might not have understood the issue in those terms at the time. (There's something almost admirable— almost—about just how much dedication some people apply to the task of poring through hard-to-find pieces of print media in search of evidence of sins committed by "problematic" individuals decades in the past. It also tells you everything you need to know about the accusers' real priorities. As Fisher says, the Vampire Castle pretends to care about structural issues but "in practice it never focuses on anything but individual behavior.") Wynn's sin with regard to Angel consisted—in total—in (a) giving him a few seconds of voice work (reading a quote from John Waters) in one of her videos and (b) refusing to denounce him when his various transgressions were brought to light. Note that she *was* willing to express her strong disagreement with his transmedicalist views. She was also willing to agree that, if he did what he's been accused of doing during his long-ago divorce, that was indeed a bad thing to do. What she wasn't willing to do was to take the extra step to say that he was a bad person for doing these bad things or that she refused to have anything to do with him in the future.

Fisher says that one of the "laws" of the Vampire Castle is to always essentialize those singled out as enemies.

While fluidity of identity, plurality and multiplicity are always claimed on behalf of the VC members—partly to cover up their own invariably wealthy, privileged or bourgeois-assimilationist background—the enemy is always to be essentialized. Since the desires animating the VC are in large part priests' desires to excommunicate and condemn, there has to be a strong distinction between Good and Evil, with the latter essentialized.

In other words, it's not good enough to express disagreement with the worst things that Buck Angel has ever done. It's necessary to agree that Angel is *defined* by those things—that he is essentially a bad person, and that he must be excommunicated.

This brings us to another point not covered by Fisher (but which re-enforces his analogy between cancel culture and vampirism): Cancelation *spreads*. To be a logic nerd about it, cancelation is "transitive." A transitive property is one such that if A has that property relative to B and B has it relative to C, A has it relative to C. You can be deemed worthy of cancelation for not canceling someone deemed worthy of cancelation—never mind whether *you've* done anything at all.

But hey, I can hear some of you saying, *Natalie Wynn is totally fine—just look at how many people still subscribe to her Patreon! And even Barbara Ehrenreich is fine. So what is everyone whining about? No one is ever really canceled.*

Three points are in order here. First, there's a massive and frankly bizarre inconsistency in the views of people who, in all sorts of other contexts, center subjective experience—"you have no idea how much emotional pain you cause non-binary people by not denouncing Buck Angel"—but who somehow think that no one has any grounds for complaint about the relentless cruelty displayed in online pile-ons if the victims of those pile-ons still have careers at the end of the process. Second, as a matter of fact, cancelation sometimes *does* end careers, as for example when the otherwise materially powerless online mobs ally themselves with the semi-feudal power of American capitalist employers by "doxing" people—i.e. ratting them out to their bosses for their online transgressions. (For a grimly hilarious example of this phenomenon look up the case of *Des Moines Register* reporter Aaron Calvin, who (a) destroyed the budding career of the 24-year-old subject of what was supposed to be a feel good story by digging up and self-righteously exposing the bigoted jokes the man had made on Twitter when he was 16, then (b) had his *own* long-forgotten bad tweets exposed by others in retaliation, (c) was fired for those tweets by the *Register*, and (d) doggedly continued through all of this to insist that "cancel culture" doesn't exist. As Slavoj Zizek might say, ideology is a hell of a drug.) Third, the "merely" emotional effects of toxic online behavior sometimes have severe real-world consequences. Mark Fisher, for example, took his own life 4 years after publishing "Exiting the Vampire Castle." He'd struggled with depression for a long time, but years of being smeared and hounded online could only have made a bad situation worse.

Of course, the mob *usually* doesn't get this kind of reward for its efforts. If "cancelation" means "being driven to suicide" or even "being so universally shunned that you're left with no supporters and no friends and no source of income," and "cancel culture" means "this sort of thing being such a big problem in society in general that it's pretty common for people to meet this fate," then "cancel culture" does not exist. But this is a silly way to argue. You can define just about any problem out of existence with sufficiently strict definitions. You might as well say that economic injustice doesn't exist in America in the twenty-first century because employees aren't generally chained to their workstations and whipped if they check their social media accounts between nine in the morning and five in the afternoon. Or that racism doesn't exist because there aren't any "whites only" signs left in restaurant windows.

"Cancel culture" refers to a cluster of cultural trends that have different levels of impact in different parts of our culture. It might be more precisely accurate to call it "denunciation culture" or "shaming culture" or some such thing, but the label is well-established—and let's remember that the "cancelers" themselves were the ones who first started calling what they were doing "canceling" people. The particular corner of our culture that I'm interested in exploring in this book is the political subculture of the left. Even without having mathematically precise information about the scope of the problem, it's a safe bet that the denunciation and shaming practices that I'll follow convention in referring to as "cancelation" are more common in this subculture than they are in e.g. the subculture of birders or the subculture of professional football.

The reason I see this as such a problem is *not* that these practices always or even usually work in isolating or destroying their targets. That's worth saying twice: *The problem with cancel culture is not that it's so effective.* In a certain sense, it's actually a bigger problem when it's *not* effective. Once more with feeling: Think not just about the positive utility of whatever you hope to accomplish but of the high probability of outcomes with extreme disutility to left-wing goals. If we denounce "problematic" comedians, and thus make ourselves look like some secular version of evangelical preachers ranting about the blasphemous undercurrents they take themselves to have detected in popular TV shows, *and* we demonstrate that all our huffing and puffing doesn't even blow these comedians' stupid little careers down, then we've succeeded in making ourselves look both spectacularly unappealing *and* completely powerless. Both halves of that are a problem if we're interested in presenting a vision of the world that a great mass of ordinary people can get excited about *and* giving them confidence that it can be achieved.

When the Committee on Public Safety in the French Revolution got so paranoid it started executing good revolutionaries like Danton, or when Stalin started filling his gulags with Old Bolsheviks, it was fair to describe what had happened as "the revolution eating its children." Some overheated commentators (especially those working right-wing grifts by trying to spook the elderly about SJWs Running Wild) like to describe internet cancel culture in the same terms. That's clearly inappropriate. The Very Online Left isn't eating its children. It's just sort of *gnawing* on them in a sad, toothless way that makes most onlookers look away with disgust. It's annoying (and can be deeply demoralizing) for the victims, but it usually doesn't hurt them in material terms. Robespierre may have become monstrous in many ways toward the end of his life (before the revolution got around to eating *him*), but as is demonstrated by the enduring popularity of guillotine jokes as a way of expressing righteous indignation against the 1 percent, his form of brutality at least had a certain kind of revolutionary sex appeal. The Very Online Left lacks even that. If the sign we're putting in our window is "ENDLESS COLLECTIVE RECRIMINATIONS THAT DON'T REALLY GO ANYWHERE—JOIN US SO WE CAN GNAW ON YOU," don't expect too many people to sign up.

8

The Genealogy of Left Moralism

In the First Essay of his book *The Genealogy of Morals*, Friedrich Nietzsche says that Dante made a "crude blunder" when he placed the inscription "I Too Was Created by Eternal Love" on the gateway to his version of hell. It would have been more accurate, Nietzsche says, if Dante had placed a sign reading "I Too Was Created by Eternal Hate" at the gates of Heaven.

Nietzsche thought the Christian vision of the afterlife reflected a sadistic desire to see sinners suffer that made a mockery of the Church's pretension to "love" sinners (while merely hating *sin*). To back up this accusation, he quotes a line from the *Summa Theologica* where St Thomas Aquinas speculates that one of the pleasures of the saved in Heaven will be a front row seat to the torments of the unsaved in hell. *In order that the bliss of the saints be more delightful for them and that they may render more copious thanks to God for it, it is given to them to see perfectly the punishment of the damned.*

In the Second Essay, Nietzsche extends this critique to the punishment of criminals in this world. He claims that the idea that the criminal *deserves* punishment because of his moral responsibility for crimes he has committed of his own "free will" is a sophisticated rationalization of a much more primitive instinct. Nietzsche thinks that we get a better insight into the emotional sources of our practices of punishment when we think hard about the claim that the criminal is punished in order to pay back his "debt" to society. Debts can only be paid back in the currency of suffering if—like Aquinas' saints in Heaven watching the torments of the damned—we *enjoy watching people suffer*. Our inherited notions of both human and divine "justice," Nietzsche suggests, are rationalizations for sadism.

Whether this line of thought is entirely correct is beside the point for my purposes here. I'm an atheist, so I have no particular interest in defending Christianity from Nietzsche's critique, but I think I can see what such a defense might look like from the perspective of a left-wing Christian thinker like Cornel West. One of West's big themes is that all religions come in "priestly" and "prophetic" forms. While he might agree that there's a sadistic streak in "priestly" Christianity—the Christianity of institutional churches that have always given their blessing to kings and conquerors—he would presumably argue that this feature isn't shared by the better "prophetic" version of the faith that, for example, inspired runaway slaves in the nineteenth century and civil rights marchers in the twentieth.

Whatever one makes of these issues, my interest here is in the use to which Mark Fisher puts Nietzsche's ideas in the Vampire Castle essay. To understand that connection, we have to start with ideas popularized by Barbara Ehrenreich, along with Adolph Reed and a few other scholars, about the role of the Professional-Managerial Class (PMC) in late capitalism.

When Karl Marx talked about the "middle class," he generally meant "the petty bourgeoise" (i.e. small business-owners). This group had class interests that didn't quite line up with the interests of the working class on the one hand or the big bourgeoise (e.g. factory-owners) on the other.

When theorists like Ehrenreich talk about the PMC, they're talking about a social group that *partially* overlaps with the "middle class" that Marx was talking about but also includes many people who are technically (highly skilled and highly paid) members of the working class. Think of, on the one hand, lawyers who are owners or co-owners of their own small firms, and on the other hand lawyers who are employees of corporations or even nonprofits or the public sector.

What the PMC all have in common is a relatively privileged social and cultural status (and usually a relatively privileged financial status) that derives from their education and credentials. If you are, like me, enough of an old-fashioned Marxist to want to reserve the word "class" for groups defined by their relationship to the means of production—i.e. whether they own businesses or they work for those who do—you can mentally substitute "caste" for "class" and continue to use the PMC acronym.

I should add that this distinction isn't just nitpicking inspired by excessive loyalty to the conceptual categories of a long-dead German economic theorist. In some situations—e.g. professors deciding whether to participate in an effort to organize the faculty of their university into a union—some people who fit into the PMC category might be torn between thinking of themselves as workers and thinking of themselves as "professionals." Telling them that they *really are* middle-class professionals and not workers isn't just technically incorrect from a Marxist standpoint. It's deeply counterproductive.

Putting this issue aside, it's undeniable that most academics, most journalists, and most other members of the PMC usually *do* think of themselves as middle-class "professionals." What drove Ehrenreich's work on this "class" was a sense that even when they didn't own their own little businesses, members of the PMC tended by virtue of their training and "professional values" (i.e. their fetishization of education and credentials) to act as go-betweens to ordinary workers on behalf of whoever *did* own the place. To see Ehrenreich's point, think about people who work at corporate HR offices conducting training on how to speak and behave in appropriately sensitive and inclusive ways. And how those same HR reps (or "diversity officers" at places with sufficiently variegated layers of bureaucracy) are then tasked with disciplining ordinary workers who get out of line.

To be clear, the existence of these rules isn't always a bad thing. (No one should have to be exposed to racial slurs at work, for example.) But there are good reasons why most people who come into contact with such offices come to resent their rigidity, excessive literalism, and tendency toward petty bureaucratic gate-keeping and zealous administration of the letter of the law. All of these features are in turn imported into the habits of the left by those who were acculturated into thinking this way before they became interested in left politics.

The analogy between the Very Online Left and corporate HR offices is strongest when the correction is being done in a polite and friendly manner. Like HR reps, people "calling in" someone guilty of a Bad Take or otherwise problematic bit of online or offline behavior generally don't feel the need to provide arguments. They don't want to give you their *reasons* for thinking you're in the wrong, let you offer your reasons for thinking you're right, and then spend some time thinking about it all. They just want to inform you of your wrongness and give you the chance to repent.

And, of course, the politeness can itself be canceled. Here's Fisher on the "tactics" of the VC:

> X has made a remark/ has behaved in a particular way—these remarks/ this behaviour might be construed as transphobic/ sexist etc. So far, OK. But it's the next move which is the kicker. X then becomes defined *as* a transphobe/ sexist etc. Their whole identity becomes defined by one ill-judged remark or behavioural slip. Once the VC has mustered its witch-hunt, the victim (often from a working class background, and not schooled in the passive aggressive etiquette of the bourgeoisie) can reliably be goaded into losing their temper, further securing their position as pariah/latest to be consumed in feeding frenzy.

The part about the "feeding frenzy" takes us from the HR Department aspect of leftist cancel culture to something a lot darker. I've been the recipient of a few Twitter pile-ons, and far more often the queasy observer of them. (I'm sure there have been times I've also been on the other end. It's easy to be inspired by someone else's expressions of anger and disgust at a Bad Tweet to add in a few expressions of anger and disgust of your own without thinking of yourself as part of a pile-on. As Jon Ronson says in *So You've Been Publicly Shamed*, no individual snowflake needs to take responsibility for an avalanche.) I've seen the process play out enough times to know that the aggression stops being "passive" as soon as the group mind has decided that the victim is essentially and irredeemably awful. At that point, anyone on the "right side" of the pile-on can say just about anything, and if you object to anything anyone says, you're guilty of "tone-policing" and siding with the guilty party. (Remember, *canceling is transitive*. If A has been canceled and B is seen as "defending" B from the mob, B might well be canceled for taking this position.) If you're a member of a group with some particular standing on this issue—if you're gay, for example, and the victim is seen as having been problematic on gay issues—then anyone trying to "shut you up" when you denounce the accused in the most over-the-top terms must be speaking from a place of heterosexual privilege and siding with your oppressors. (If the person objecting to the toxic pile-on is *also gay*, then don't worry, the VC has the conceptual resources to make sense of that. They're full of helpful explanations along the lines of *gay people can also be homophobic*.) If you *aren't* part of a group with relevant standing on the issue, you perform your virtue as an "ally" by finding over-the-top and vile things to say about the victim.

In her excellent video "Canceling," Natalie Wynn displays on the screen and reads off a small sample of the tweets that filled her timeline for months after the Buck Angel controversy broke. For several minutes, viewers see every possible variation of "f--- Natalie," "Natalie is a f---ing grifter," "f--- Natalie and f—her f—ing grift," "Natalie is truscum" (this last being a slang term for Buck Angel's "transmedicalist" position), "anyone still defending Natalie is f---ing truscum," "Natalie is a truscum TERF," "Natalie should be deplatformed," etc., etc., etc. Most tellingly, not all of the tweets even get the names of the principals right. At least one calls Buck Angel "Angel Buck," which as Wynn notes in her video goes to show that they literally *hadn't even heard of* the object of their outrage before the pile-on started.

What's going on there? To help understand the structure of the situation, imagine that a citizen of a fundamentalist theocracy is condemned to death by stoning. The set-up works like this: Some priestly tribunal conducts the actual trial, weighs the evidence, and pronounces the sentence. At that point, the rules of this particular theocracy allow any random citizen to prove their patriotism and piety by picking up a stone. Some of those who answer the call may not be quite sure what the accused did or even who they are. (See "Angel Buck.") So why do they participate in the stoning? Genuine ideological conviction is often part of the answer. Many people trust that the tribunal knows what it's doing. As Winston Smith reassures himself in the final pages of *1984*, after he's repented his past ideological lapses, "the Party was in the right. It must be so..." But this isn't a complete explanation. Any psychologically realistic assessment of their motives is also going to include the dimension that Nietzsche focused on—that throwing stones can be cathartic and fun. The two motives often reinforce each other. You can enjoy your sadistic pleasures with a clean conscience if you truly believe that the victim had it coming.

Inside the walls of the VC, everyone tends to avoid talking about how much fun they're having when they denounce and shame allegedly deserving victims. After all, once you've admitted *that*, you pretty much have to concede that there's a tremendous psychological incentive to nurture and exaggerate small grievances (so you have a *justification* for throwing stones), to search for and emphasize subtle respects in which you're oppressed (so you have *standing* to throw stones), and to ignore anything that might complicate your understanding of the victim's alleged transgression (so you aren't *talked out* of throwing stones).

While I think that Fisher's class analysis is basically correct, it's worth noting that class-as-a-marker-of-individual-identity can all too easily be assimilated into the VC framework. It can be fun for *anyone* to throw stones, and this includes people from economically disadvantaged backgrounds weaponizing their "lived experience" to give them standing in cancelation games with comrades from PMC backgrounds. There are also online socialists who like to make hair-trigger accusations that every leftist they dislike or disagree with about anything is a "neoliberal grifter" and a practitioner of "idpol" (identity politics). To borrow a phrase from my *Dead Pundits Society* co-host Adam Proctor, people like this have set up shop in the *basement* of the Vampire Castle, replicating all the toxic features of standard left-wing cancel culture while telling themselves that they're vampire hunters. Fisher's failure to see that the VC could easily mutate in these directions is one of the few flaws in his otherwise brilliant analysis. Even so, his essay gives us the conceptual tools to understand both the original VC and the basement version.

One of Fisher's most fascinating claims is made in passing.

[T]he VC has recourse to all the infernal strategies, dark pathologies and psychological torture instruments Christianity invented, and which Nietzsche described in *The Genealogy of Morals*. This priesthood of bad conscience, this nest of pious guilt-mongers, is exactly what Nietzsche predicted when he said that something worse than Christianity was already on the way. Now, here it is...

He never explains this or expands on the line of thought. It would be easy to dismiss it as hyperbole. The "instruments of psychological torture" devised by the Christian Church have been used to horrible effect in a variety of situations spanning 2 millennia—recent "greatest hits" include Ireland's Magdalene Laundries and American evangelical "conversion therapy" for gay teenagers, and those aren't even the worst items on the list. What could it mean to say that left-wing cancel culture is worse?

If he means "worse in concrete consequences," then the claim is almost certainly false. Cancelation really does inflict serious psychological damage on some people, and you can certainly argue—as I do—that left-wing cancel culture has very bad *indirect* consequences by virtue of making it harder for the left to change the world for the better. But it would still be a bit much to claim that it's responsible for worse things than that litany of horrors. If nothing else, the online cancel mobs would have trouble competing with the historical record of the church without achieving state power and keeping it for centuries.

Here's an alternate reading of Fischer's point: The Vampire Castle is worse than Christianity in the sense that it drops the pretense to love sinners (and merely hate the sin).

Even if everything Nietzsche says about Christian hypocrisy in *The Genaeology of Morals* is spot-on, it doesn't follow that dispensing with that hypocrisy is a good thing. Compare: Capitalism relies on the pretense that the subordination of workers to unelected bosses doesn't violate their freedom because workers "freely" agree to this arrangement when they sign employment contracts. The reality is that, since most people aren't in any realistic position to start a business of their own they have no realistic long-term choice but to either accept a job where they'll be subordinated to unelected bosses or to live in misery on the fringes of society. (Investors and small business loans can be hard to come by, and the vast majority of people from working-class backgrounds who do manage to start businesses for a while fail and end up back in the working class.) Even in a tight labor market where it's easy to get a new job, workers only get to choose between different bosses. They have a boss one way or the other. Plutocrats who celebrate capitalist economic "freedom" while enriching themselves through the labor of workers who are working under conditions they never would have accepted if they had a reasonable alternative are hypocrites. Nevertheless, if this hypocrisy were dropped and workers were made the legal property of their employers, that would be a lot worse. Similarly, rich people have a lot more political power than poor people, so the idea that democratic-but-capitalist governments represent all citizens equally is absurd, but it would be bad if the greater political power of rich people were codified by formally disenfranchising the poor.

An official piety of a system can be somewhat hypocritical while also doing real good in limiting that system's worst aspects. It's good that workers have a right to quit and that poor people have a right to vote. And it's good that Christianity at least pretended to cherish sinners.

Most leftists are officially committed to the position that even imprisoned rapists and murderers should be treated more compassionately. Even those of us who don't go around calling ourselves "prison abolitionists" think that people who've committed these crimes should be serving shorter terms in more humane prisons with a greater focus on rehabilitation. Yet somehow far too many of us are comfortable with the idea that enthusiastically cruel social shaming should be the standard punishment for Bad Takes and problematic jokes.

Like many leftists, I spent years harboring many of these complaints about the left without talking about them very much. My thinking went something like this: *We live in a world with imperialist wars and runaway climate change, with police brutality and union-busting and staggering levels of economic inequality. Given the existence of all of those problems, who cares about the flaws and foibles of the left? Let's get our priorities straight!*

I still think that's a good response to the Dave Rubins of the world, who use the existence of uptight scolds and pedants on the left to justify joining the right wing and defending an indefensible status quo but I no longer think it's an adequate reason for leftists not to engage in intra-left critique. One reason is what we can call The Lady Bird Response.

In the 2017 movie *Lady Bird*, the title character—teenage Christine "Lady Bird" McPherson—has a fight with her boyfriend. The boyfriend is a Chomsky-reading leftist. When Christine starts to complain about how he's handled their relationship he icily tells her that a million people died in Iraq. Her response is that *more than one thing can be bad.*

When censorious Twitter mobs gang up on someone for a tweet taken out of context and people spew all sorts of toxic nonsense at the victim, the fact that vastly worse things are going on in the world isn't a good enough reason not to tell everyone to knock it off. Even if the only reason to tell them to stop is that they're being cruel and people shouldn't treat each other that way—even when nothing much material is at stake—that's a good enough reason to do so. *More than one thing can be bad.*

An even more important reason the left pathologies I've been calling attention to in this book deserve our attention is that, as I've tried to show, that way of doing things is deeply counterproductive. And the fact that a big chunk of the behavior I'm talking about is "just online" can no longer be taken as an excuse.

As I'm writing these lines, the coronavirus pandemic has shut down big chunks of the global economy. If you have a job that can be done online, your employer has probably handed you a laptop and sent you home. Several states have legally ordered their residents to "shelter in place." Everything from street protests to door-to-door political canvassing is currently inconsistent with the guidelines issued by the Centers for Disease Control.

That means that for an indeterminate number of months, the

only place that left-wing political persuasion can take place is Online. It means that the "oh, stop taking Online so seriously, just log off your social media accounts and take a run" excuse has been suspended for the duration of the emergency.

But here's the thing: Even when things return to whatever "normal" is going to look like now, we shouldn't return to brushing off Online as if it weren't an important sphere of political persuasion. As if the same pathologies didn't manifest themselves offline as online. And as if it weren't the case that the way the left presents itself matters to whether ordinary people find us appealing enough to want to stick around to listen to what we have to say.

The more we present ourselves as moralistic hall monitors, the harder it is for us to win over the masses of ordinary people we need to convince in order for us to have any chance of doing much of anything about those imperialist wars and all the rest of the high-priority problems listed above. And that is itself a high-priority problem.

I've been framing my critique of the current iteration of the left in strategic terms throughout this book, but what I worry most about is that far too many leftists don't bother thinking about strategic issues at all because, even if they aren't fully conscious of this, they don't take seriously the possibility that they *could* win. Instead, they see their role as simply "taking a stand" against forces too powerful to ever actually be defeated.

When politics becomes a moral performance, the question of whether or not you're actually advancing your stated goals recedes into the background. You see your political commitments the way Immanuel Kant saw his system of deontological morality. "A good will," Kant wrote in his *Groundwork for the Metaphysics of Morals*, "is good not because of what it effects, or accomplishes, not because of its fitness to attain some intended end, but good just by its willing, i.e. in itself." Even if it "accomplished nothing" it would still "shine like a jewel" as "something that has full worth in itself."

I prefer the view of Karl Marx, who wrote about a century later in his *Theses on Feurbach* that "previous philosophers have only interpreted the world." The point, he said, is to change it.

Links to Some of the Articles Discussed in This Book

"Exiting the Vampire Castle" by Mark Fisher
https://www.opendemocracy.net/en/opendemocracyuk/exiting-vampire-castle/

"The Beginning of the End of Capitalist Realism" by Micah Uetricht
https://jacobinmag.com/2019/01/capitalist-realism-mark-fisher-k-punk-depression

"The Myth of Class Reductionism" by Adolph Reed
https://newrepublic.com/article/154996/myth-class-reductionism

"From Jenner to Dolezal" by Adolph Reed
https://www.commondreams.org/views/2015/06/15/jenner-dolezal-one-trans-good-other-not-so-much

"What Does Identitarian Deference Require?" by Matt Bruenig
http://mattbruenig.com/2013/02/26/what-does-identitarian-deference-require/

"On the Origins of the Professional-Managerial Class: An Interview with Barbara Ehrenreich" by Alex Press
https://www.dissentmagazine.org/online_articles/on-the-origins-of-the-professional-managerial-class-an-interview-with-barbara-ehrenreich

"Blunt Instruments" by Christopher Hitchens
Prepared for the Worst: Selected Essays and Minority Reports by Christopher Hitchens

"Dave Chappelle and Comedy" by Ralph Leonard
https://areomagazine.com/2019/11/13/dave-chappelle-and-comedy/

"It's Good That Joe Rogan Endorsed Bernie. Now We Have to Organize" by Michael Brooks and Ben Burgis
https://www.jacobinmag.com/2020/01/its-good-that-joe-rogan-endorsed-bernie-now-we-have-to-organize

"Kronstadt – Once More" by Victor Serge
https://www.marxists.org/archive/serge/1938/04/kronstadt.htm

"Marx Deserves Better Critics" by Ben Burgis
https://quillette.com/2019/04/24/marx-deserves-better-critics/

"The Left Can't Just Dismiss the Anti-Lockdown Protests" by Ben Burgis
https://www.jacobinmag.com/2020/04/coronavirus-pandemic-lockdown-protests-ubi

"Writing Behind Enemy Lines" by Ben Burgis
https://www.patreon.com/posts/36138344

"How Zizek Should Have Replied to Jordan Peterson: A Missed Opportunity to Respond to Facile Critiques of Socialism" by Benjamin Studebaker
https://www.currentaffairs.org/2019/04/how-zizek-should-have-replied-to-jordan-peterson

"Exclusive: We Found Archie Carter" by Aaron Freedman
https://www.jacobinmag.com/2019/08/archie-carter-quillette-dsa

"What the Media Missed at the Jordan Peterson-Slavoj Zizek Debate" by Clifton Mark
https://www.canadalandshow.com/what-media-missed-at-the-jordan-peterson-slavoj-zizek-debate/

"Discipline, Strategy and Morality: Or Why Beating Up Unarmed Writers is a Poor Way to Advance Left-Wing Ideas" by Nathan Robinson
https://www.currentaffairs.org/2019/07/discipline-strategy-and-morality

"Why Charles Murray is Odious" by Nathan Robinson
https://www.currentaffairs.org/2017/07/why-is-charles-murray-odious

"Academics Cannot Evade Their Public Responsibilities" by Nathan Robinson
https://www.currentaffairs.org/2019/09/academics-cannot-evade-their-public-responsibilities

Appendix: NYC-DSA Cancels Adolph Reed as Police Stations Burn

A few months after I wrote that last chapter, New York City DSA was planning to co-sponsor a Zoom lecture by Adolph Reed on "racial disparity ideology." The immediate context was the COVID-19 pandemic. Many left-wing commentators and progressive politicians had been pointing out that the pandemic was killing black people at a much higher rate than it was killing the white population. Very few had spelled out the *reason* why this was the case.

One reason Reed found this trend disturbing was that he was concerned it could give "racial medicine" a new lease of life. Clusters of genetic features associated with common ancestry that sometimes at least loosely correlate with conventional ideas about "race" *can* be medically relevant in some contexts but Professor Reed has long been concerned that an overemphasis on race-based medical explanations can provide allegedly "scientific" cover to the long-discredited idea that "race" is a natural genetic category rather than a socially constructed one.

His main complaint, though, was about the ways that racism-per-se is an incomplete social and historical explanation of both the disparity in COVID deaths and various other racial disparities. By far the most important reason that black people were dying of the virus at a higher rate than white people was that, due to America's history of *de jure* racial apartheid, black people were far more likely to live in poverty than white people and *poor people* were far more likely than middle-class or affluent people to be killed by the virus for extremely obvious reasons ranging from having worse medical care to being far less likely to be able to work from home. The reasons Reed thought this point deserved emphasis were that (a) an explanation of the disparity that centered on poverty more precisely captured the underlying empirical facts and (b) such an explanation was more likely to be politically useful in assembling the broadest possible political coalition to combat the source of the problem.

NYC-DSA canceled its sponsorship of the event under intense pressure from those members who thought Reed was a "class reductionist" or somehow hostile to the anti-racist cause. In particular, many of Reed's critics within DSA thought it was outrageous to hold such an event in the middle of the intense nationwide unrest sparked by the police murder of George Floyd.

Floyd was a working-class black man who'd lost his job due to the pandemic. He was arrested for paying for cigarettes with a counterfeit $20 bill and killed by the arresting officer, who held his knee on Floyd's neck for eight minutes and forty-six seconds as Floyd begged for his life. In the subsequent national outpouring of fury that followed this grotesque act of state violence, a police station in Minneapolis was burned to the ground. Protests spread and police around the country seemed almost to be trying their best to remind everyone of why people were so angry at them. There were innumerable incidents of police teargassing peaceful protestors, trapping protestors on bridges and then brutalizing them for not following orders to go home, attacking journalists even after they'd seen press passes, covering up badges so they couldn't be reported, blinding protestors by firing rubber bullets directly into their faces, and on and on like that in a seemingly endless list of abuses.

Anyone who wasn't the worst kind of apologist for arbitrary power would be outraged by all of this. But did any of it add up to a reason to oppose a lecture by a fierce lifelong critic of racial and economic injustice? No one who knew anything about Reed would think he would be on the side of the police.

Some of Reed's detractors in DSA "just" called for the event to be turned into a debate, although (i) they typically didn't even bother to say *who* Reed should debate, (ii) this demand for a change of format was being raised far too close to the planned time of the event to be realistic, and (iii) it's extremely doubtful that if Reed's views on these matters were closer to their own they would have found it inappropriate for him to have the online stage to himself for an hour before opening up the floor to Q&As. I'm a big believer in the value of debate, but the idea it was *only* acceptable for NYC-DSA to hear from this allegedly "problematic" speaker if someone was sharing the spotlight with him and reassuring the audience that he's wrong strikes me as a fairly clumsy attempt to split the difference between those DSA members who would have liked to hear what Reed had to say and those who just wanted him to shut up.

In any case, as far as I know, NYC-DSA never offered Reed the option of turning his scheduled lecture into a debate. They simply pulled their sponsorship. And the online pile-on against Reed and the event organizers had become sufficiently toxic in the hours leading up to that decision that the lecture ended up being canceled outright out of concern that "Zoom-bombers" would disrupt the event.

The irony of an overwhelmingly white organization canceling a black Marxist academic in the name of "anti-racism" doesn't need to be labored. But two related points do deserve to be emphasized.

The first is that this incident says a lot about the limits of the politics of "deferring to oppressed people." No one took a poll of the non-white members of NYC-DSA to see how many thought the organization should withdraw its sponsorship of the event. It was just taken for granted that those black DSA members trying to cancel a black socialist visiting speaker were speaking for "the" black point of view on the matter and a great many white DSA members—surely the majority of the cancelers in this case—took this as a reason to join the pile-on.

This speaks to a larger problem diagnosed by Matt Bruenig in his 2013 essay "What Does Identitarian Deference Require?"

If you want to suspend your own judgment about some issue and defer to the opinions of the oppressed, first you need to figure out who speaks for the oppressed. Bruenig cites a Gallop poll according to which 44 percent of women identify as pro-life and 50 percent identify as pro-choice. It's clearly not possible to defer to women in general on this topic. Is the six-point gap good enough to take pro-choice women as speaking for women as a category? What if the figures were reversed? It's not exactly impossible to imagine political and cultural changes that would turn the 44 percent into 51 percent. Would that mean that "men shouldn't have anything to say about abortion, they should just listen to women" would now entail that men should just shut up and listen to pro-life women? Of course, you could have a good independent argument for the conclusion that abortion restrictions unjustly oppress women—and to be clear, I believe that we *do* have such arguments—but as Bruenig points out, if you're relying on such an argument you're *not* suspending your own judgment in order to defer to the opinion of women. All the same considerations would apply to this case even *if* someone had done a poll of black DSA members in New York and found that most of them disagreed with Reed. And again: No one did that.

The second and more important point is that Reed's critics were treating the issue as one of anti-racism vs. indifference to racism, as if Reed were some black conservative opponent of Affirmative Action, rather than acknowledging that at least two competing visions of anti-racism were at play in the debate. According to one, race and class are two independently explanatory variables that "intersect" in various ways. White people oppress black people and bosses oppress workers and the two forms of oppression may intersect in complicated ways in any given scenario but they're basically two different "structures." (What using the word "structural" in this case means if not a reference to either civil and legal inequality a la Jim Crow or the devastating long-term economic effects of those inequalities is not always clear. The idea sometimes just seems to be that people in positions of power act on the basis of racial bias.) According to the other vision of anti-racism, racial disparities that remain after civic and legal inequalities have been stamped out need to be addressed on a primarily economic level. Racial biases may have all sorts of effects within the psychology of any individual decision-maker but if we're talking about contemporary social *structures* "race" doesn't explain much by itself. If you're getting ready to dismiss this as "class reductionism," remember that the key phrase is "by itself." Here's the idea:

Take the kind of aggressive, violent, and increasingly militarized policing that claimed the life of George Floyd. Black people are vastly more likely than white people to end up on the receiving end of police violence, and that has everything to do with America's horrifying racial history, but you haven't really explained the problem until you fill in the middle link in that chain of causation. The result of America's apartheid history is that black people are far more likely than white people to be *poor*, and aggressive, violent, militarized policing is a general problem afflicting poor neighborhoods. Part of the reason that black people are more likely to be shot by the police than white people is the conscious or unconscious racial biases of many policemen, but even if all such bias could be magically eliminated tomorrow, black people would be more likely than white people to be victims of police shootings because *poor people* are more likely than middle-class or affluent people to be victims.

The reluctance by many leftists to emphasize this point is powerful evidence of the extent to which politics has been reduced to a performance of moral commitment on the contemporary left. White leftists often feel that the more they emphasize the racial dimension of the police violence problem, the more they're displaying their identification with the category of the population that's most victimized by the kind of policing that currently exists. But when we frame police violence in exclusively racial terms, the message that we send to poor white people whose interests would be served by rolling back police militarization is *don't worry, this problem won't impact you, this is only a problem of those other people over there.* That's not a good way to win.

Some leftists like to talk about "fighting the good fight." I hate that phrase. Life is short. There are mountains to climb and philosophical texts to grapple with and sexual relationships to pursue and friends to spend time with and music to listen to and whiskey to drink. These things are all a lot more fun than marching through the streets shouting about police violence and hoping the cops don't decide to give you an in-person demonstration of the problem. Why bother with the "good fight" if you aren't going to fight to win?

Bonus Essay on *Jacobin* and *Quillette*: The Ballad of Archie Carter

(Revised and expanded from "Writing Behind Enemy Lines," originally published at patreon.com/benburgis)

I usually prefer to strategically critique left-wing cancel culture without leaning too hard on examples drawn from my own experience but it would be silly to pretend that (a) I don't have any such experience or that (b) it wasn't on my mind while I was writing the book. I'll give two examples here.

One had to do with an article I wrote for my usual publisher, *Jacobin*, about a protest against the coronavirus "lockdown" that happened in my home state of Michigan. In the piece I argued that the protestors' demand that the shelter in place orders be lifted before the public health crisis passed was irresponsible. My brother and sister were both born at Lansing's Sparrow Hospital—I was born a few minutes away at St Lawrence— and I used to pass by Sparrow on my way to classes at Lansing Community College. I was viscerally horrified to see photographs of a doctor in a white coat wandering out into the street to plead with a contingent of Proud Boys who were stopping ambulances from getting in and out of the hospital by blockading a nearby intersection. I said in *Jacobin* that some of the specific grievances about lawn supply stores and haircuts mentioned by protestors quoted in mainstream articles were ludicrously petty. I expressed my deep lack of sympathy for business-owners who wanted to force their employees back to work by cutting off their unemployment benefits as the pandemic continued to rage. I also pointed out that polling at the time showed that the protestors currently represented a "distinct Trumpian minority" and that the organizations behind the protest were less "grassroots" than billionaire-funded astroturf. If I'd stopped there my article probably wouldn't have been especially controversial.

Instead, in the last section of the article I pointed out that even some protestors who were members of what I called "thuggish right-wing organizations" were articulating legitimate economic grievances about issues like mortgage and car payments. I argued that even if the protests *currently* didn't have much support there was a real danger that their movement might start to gain wider popular support if the lockdowns dragged on too much longer without much more serious economic relief for ordinary people. I said that instead of responding to the protestors in a way that began and ended with making fun of them the left should focus on undercutting their arguments by fighting for at least a temporary Universal Basic Income and a forgiveness for all rent and mortgage payments for the duration of the crisis. A lockdown plus a UBI plus rent forgiveness struck me as far more politically viable than a lockdown plus paltry unemployment benefits for those who even qualify for them.

The resulting pile-on was a wonder to behold. Some of the highest profile pilers-on were liberals like Matthew Yglesias and *Nation* contributor Joshua Holland but there were also a whole horde of Twitter users with the democratic socialist rose emoji in their handles accusing me of "falling for astroturf" or even supporting a socialist/fascist "red-brown alliance." The anti-war left in the Bush era didn't have any trouble understanding that when people like Noam Chomsky and Glenn Greenwald pointed out that a lot of terrorism was caused by blowback from US interventions around the world and that this is a reason to oppose such interventions they weren't expressing sympathy for Al Queda. Somehow, though, all these comrades thought my advocacy of *taking away the lockdown protestors' best recruitment pitch by providing better solutions to the economic grievances they were articulating* amounted to "support" for the protests.

A previous example had to do with a debate held in Toronto in 2019 between self-help guru and right-wing commentator Jordan

Peterson and Slovenian Marxist intellectual Slavoj Zizek. Full-disclosure: Zizek wrote the introduction to *Myth and Mayhem: A Leftist Critique of Jordan Peterson,* a book I co-wrote with Matt McManus, Marion Trejo, and Conrad Hamilton. I obviously have a bias. But more than a few observers who started with the opposite bias thought that Professor Peterson embarrassed himself.

Peterson started his opening presentation by admitting that (a) he hadn't bothered to read any of Zizek's books in preparation for the debate but that (b) he *did* go back and read Marx, because he figured "that's where the trouble started," that (c) the only Marx he'd read was *The Communist Manifesto* and finally that (d) the middle-aged Peterson was reading that extremely thin pamphlet for just the second time in his life, the first time having been when he was *18 years old.* Remember, this is a guy who's spent the last few years going around the world denouncing Marxism (or whatever he understands "Marxism" to be). The rest of his opening presentation can only be described as a bad high school book report on the *Manifesto.*

If what Zizek had wanted out of the confrontation was the adulation of already-convinced leftists, he would have taken this as an opening to rhetorically rip Peterson from limb to limb. (Benjamin Studebaker laid out some of what that might have looked like in a *Current Affairs* piece called "How Zizek Should Have Replied to Jordan Peterson.") I know I would have loved to see that, not least because Peterson would have hated every moment of it.

I'm pretty sure that's why he turned down an earlier invitation to debate Richard Wolff. Peterson's response to *that* invitation, immortalized on YouTube, was to rant and rave about Stalinism—even though Wolff's radically democratic vision of a post-capitalist society is poles apart from the one-party authoritarianism of the old Soviet Union—and to suggest that (i) advocating any form of Marxism was morally on a par with defending Hitler's "National Socialism" and that (ii) such a position was so far outside of the boundaries of acceptable discourse that he didn't want to legitimize Wolff by debating him.

What makes all of this particularly odd is that Zizek is noticeably *less* passionate than Wolff is about the importance of democracy. In a thought-provoking lecture entitled "A Plea for Bureaucratic Socialism," Zizek points out that if we brought *everything* under participatory democratic control, we'd have to waste much of our lives in meetings about things like the management of water and electric services that most of us would rather not have to think about at all. He's no more a Stalinist than Wolff is—in fact, he was a democratic dissident in the Communist Party of Slovenia in the 1980s—but, where Wolff is a happy warrior for socialism, Zizek is the kind of intellectual who's most comfortable when he's excavating the connections between ideas through layers of irony and ambiguity. So: If the association between Marxism and gulags was too strong for Peterson to be willing to debate Wolff, why did he want to debate Zizek?

Part of the answer may be financial. Peterson knew that Zizek was a bigger name and a bigger draw than Wolff. Toronto's scalpers were reportedly charging more for tickets to Zizek/ Peterson than they did for Maple Leafs tickets, and people around the world paid to see the livestream. While Zizek donated his half of the proceeds to a charity for indigenous Canadians, Peterson pocketed his. Beyond this, though, I'm fairly sure that part of the difference is that Peterson found Zizek's persona a lot less threatening. Zizek has a thick accent. He compulsively tugs on his shirt and rubs his nose. He jumps from subject to subject, making odd and amusing connections between ideas at rhetorical right angles, and he's fond of making ambiguous and intentionally provocative remarks. Peterson may have thought that nothing that happened in a conversation with someone like that would embarrass him.

If so, he was very wrong. Peterson often rants about the evils of "postmodern Marxism," which he sees as the root of identity politics and political correctness. Standard leftist responses to Peterson—including some that I've written—savage him on this point, stressing that postmodernism and Marxism are *very* different schools of thought and arguing that Peterson's conflation of them is bizarre. (Marxism is not only exactly the *kind of* "grand narrative" that post-structuralists like Derrida and Foucault were reacting against, it's the primary "grand narrative" that some of those thinkers had in mind!) Zizek's response was simpler. He asked Peterson who *exactly* he was talking about, and patiently waited...as Peterson tried and failed to come up with a single name.

All of that could only have been very embarrassing for Peterson and his most hardcore fans, but Zizek's purpose was never to "destroy" Peterson. He gently corrected a few of Peterson's many misinterpretations of Marx and Marxism and—almost as an afterthought—gave Peterson a quick recommended reading list, but he never went in for the kill. He understood that many of Peterson's followers weren't hardened reactionaries so much as confused young men looking for direction and turned off by a left that they saw as humorless and controlling, obsessed with privilege-checking and guilt-tripping (everything Mark Fisher was talking about in "Exiting the Vampire Castle"). Zizek set out to present them with a more appealing version of leftism—one far more concerned with changing the world for the better than with moralistic condemnation of individuals.

Many left-wing writers seemed dismayed that Zizek was playing so nicely with Peterson, and completely misunderstood the part where Peterson and Zizek seemed to be agreeing with each other about "political correctness." The best analysis of what happened at the Sony Center came from Canadian writer Clifton Mark.

While both are critical of political correctness (whatever they mean by it), there is a fundamental difference between their critiques that is easy to overlook. Peterson thinks the problem with political correctness is that it undermines the natural hierarchies of competence that order our world. Zizek thinks the problem is that political correctness can distract us from the economic and social hierarchies that most require undermining. Peterson attacks it from the right, Zizek from the left.

To be fair, Zizek could have done more to clarify the difference between the two critiques. It wouldn't have taken much. A few clarificatory statements between nose rubs — "my God, I am not saying that gay and trans people are not mistreated, this is not the point..." — would have gone a long way toward reassuring those on the left who didn't get what he was doing. That said, what Zizek *did* do was impressive and important. Clifton Mark's summary was excellent.

Despite the collegiality, the exchange was unequal. Peterson's expertise is in clinical psychology, not in politics, philosophy, or economics. Zizek's expertise was directly related to the topics of discussion. This made the evening feel like an office hours session between a professor and an earnest but misguided student. Zizek probed and corrected and suggested supplementary reading. But he encouraged Peterson by highlighting points of agreement, cracking jokes (literally begging Peterson to do the same), and trying to find ways to criticize without humiliating.

Immediately after the debate, I wrote an article for the right-wing journal *Quillette* entitled "Karl Marx Deserves Better Critics." I argued that Peterson's shallow and uninformed critique of Marxism made the debate less valuable, both for Marxists like me who wanted to learn from sharp criticism and for anti-Marxists who wanted to see their views well-represented on the stage in Toronto, than it would have been if Peterson had done his homework. My calculation was that even right-wing *Quillette* editors could see the merits of this narrow argument—these guys do, after all, think of themselves as intellectuals—and that, in the course of contrasting Marx's real ideas to the crude strawmen constructed by Peterson in his opening presentation, I could in effect proselytize for socialism deep in enemy territory.

I had one additional motivation for sending my write-up of the debate to *Quillette* rather than to a more ideological congenial publication—one that I'll admit is fairly petty. Jordan Peterson is a regular *Quillette* reader. (At any rate, he tweets out links to their articles on a regular basis.) My hope was that he would read my piece and be annoyed by it. I don't know if that happened. But I do know that the comment section was full of angry readers who wanted to know why editor Claire Lehmann had allowed such vile communist garbage to be published in her magazine.

Some self-righteous online leftists had the opposite concern. They liked my piece well enough, but thought I was betraying the anti-*Quillette* cause by publishing it there. In failing to adhere to what I saw as a profoundly self-sabotaging taboo against going into enemy territory to make leftist arguments, I was "legitimizing" *Quillette* and giving it credibility.

To give this critique a bit more bite, people who make it often exaggerate *Quillette*'s dominant editorial politics—which really are quite bad and reactionary—by calling it "fascist" or by playing up some of the pieces they've published defending Charles Murray's claims about race and IQ. I've seen more than a few angry Twitter leftists calling *Quillette* "the Journal of Skull-Measuring Studies" or some variation on that phrase. While I agree with the underlying critique of *Quillette*'s IQ articles—I regard Murray as a bigot and a peddler of junk science, and would strongly recommend Nathan J. Robinson's classic *Current Affairs* article "Why is Charles Murray So Odious?" for an analytically rigorous presentation of that case—these descriptions miss the mark. Put together every article they've published that has anything to do with IQ and related subjects and we're probably talking about 2 percent of what's appeared on the website. The great majority of what you'll find there on any given day is "crazy SJWs shouting down visiting speakers on college campuses" stuff—i.e. pretty standard culture war material from what's basically a center-right libertarian perspective. The reason the difference matters is that (a) if we just mindlessly call every shade of right-winger a Nazi, we give persuadable people the impression that we don't have a response to what they're *actually* saying, and (b) figuring out which of our ideological opponents are which is tactically and strategically important. Someone who's reading an actually fascist website—say, *The Daily Stormer*—is a whole lot less likely to be persuadable than someone who's drifted a bit to the right because of culture-war-based irritation with the excesses of performative wokeness.

A slightly more sophisticated objection to writing for *Quillette* I sometimes ran into went like this: *You might imagine that you're undermining their right-wing agenda by going into their territory and making left-wing arguments, but you're fooling yourself. They wouldn't publish those articles if they didn't know that doing so would ultimately serve that agenda.*

That sounds plausible until you realize that a hidden premise of this argument is that anyone who works as an editor at a right-wing magazine must *know* whether my writing an article for them that undermines their worldview and them publishing it helps their cause more than it hurts it, whereas naïve leftists like me can only guess. But why should we assume that?

Certainly, when I look at *Quillette's* decision last year to publish an article called "DSA is Doomed," allegedly written by a "Marxist-Leninist" construction worker and Mets fan named "Archie Carter," I don't get the sense that everyone who works for the magazine is a tactical and strategic genius. Here's the opening paragraph:

> I am working class and a Marxist-Leninist. I believe in a revolution of the proletariat, and the usurpation of the ruling class. As I looked around the political landscape after Donald Trump's election win, I noticed the Democratic Socialists of America (DSA). Curious, and hoping for a radical and viable alternative to the two establishment parties, I took myself along to a meeting. While DSA do not perfectly align with my politics, I became a dues-paying member all the same, attracted by the party's subversive potential. I attended meetings of the Brooklyn DSA chapter, and participated in many NYC-DSA actions—sit-ins, marches, labor protests— because of my steadfast belief in the transformative power of solidarity. I would approach political activity with this maxim in mind: what would Alinsky do?

As soon as I got to the end of that paragraph, I knew that "Archie Carter" wasn't who he said he was. This didn't take any special insight on my part. I'm pretty sure that anyone with an even passing knowledge of the socialist left as it actually exists smelled bullshit—even if they didn't put it together that the name "Archie Carter" was a combination of Archie Bunker and DSA member and Virginia state legislator Lee Carter. My guess at the time was that Carter was the only socialist whose name the author knew. Putting that aside, the real tell—the thing you have to know almost literally nothing about this stuff not to pick up on—was that this supposed "Marxist-Leninist" was a giant fan of the community organizing guru Saul Alinsky. Right-wing conspiracy theorists are obsessed with Alinsky. Most leftists only have a vague idea of who he is, and the few Marxists who've devoted more than a passing thought to Alinsky tend to be critics of his brand of liberal local activism. "Carter" returns to Alinsky in the final lines of the piece:

> If DSA wants to transform America into the country that Saul Alinsky envisioned, then it needs to listen to America's working class. At the moment, its members are hardly aware that it exists.

My initial assumption was that the article was written by a right-winger with a hazy and ill-informed idea of what leftists sound like. I was wrong. "Archie Carter" was a leftist prankster. Within a day of his article going up on *Quillette*, *Jacobin* had tracked down the real author, who told them he picked *Quillette* for the hoax "because they would have a lower standard of proof."

...which they pretty clearly did. The only details he provides about Brooklyn DSA meetings were already a matter of public record because of profiles of the organization published in other media outlets. The correspondence screenshotted in the *Jacobin* article shows that *Quillette* asked "Carter" for proof of ID. He ignored this request. They were so eager to believe him that they published the piece anyway. Even more indefensibly, some of their editorial changes arguably crossed the line from changing the way that "Carter" *described* his fabricated experiences to *adding new fabrications*—e.g. in a passage describing what went on at DSA meetings the sentence "My union friends were horrified" was added by a *Quillette* editor.

The fictional Carter is a mash-up of dated blue-collar New York stereotypes. I'd imagine that he eats a lot of hot dogs, and that he refers to them as "dogs." I'm certain that he loudly and happily banters with other neighborhood characters as he walks down the street.

At least one *actual* blue-collar laborer has written for *Quillette*— freelance writer and Amazon warehouse worker Kevin Mims. A few weeks before "DSA is Doomed" appeared in and was then yanked from *Quillette*'s website, Mims published an article there entitled "Tourist Journalism vs. the Working Class."

In it, Mims responds to a John Oliver segment about Amazon's horrifying working conditions. I'm fairly sure that if Archie Carter really existed he would find Mims' defense of the bosses *depressing as shit*.

According to Oliver, among the indignities that the company has heaped upon its workforce are two separate instances in which a canister of bear repellant leaked in an Amazon warehouse. Oliver and his journalistic team also found former Amazon employees willing to complain on camera about working conditions in the company's warehouses and fulfillment centers: they can get very hot in the summer and very cold in the winter; getting to the bathrooms sometimes requires a long walk; pregnant women get no special bathroom accommodations.

Oliver's researchers even uncovered an incident in which a worker had died on the job and her co-workers were told to carry on working in the presence of her corpse. Amazon disputes much of this, but I have no difficulty believing that incidents like these do occasionally occur. Amazon employs approximately 650,000 people worldwide. That number is higher than the populations of 50 of the world's 233 countries. It's entirely possible that at some point a citizen of Luxembourg (population 602,000) has been sprayed by bear repellant, or that workers somewhere in Iceland (360,000) have been required to work around a fallen co-worker. But neither of these things, if they happened, would be proof that working conditions in Luxembourg or Iceland are appalling.

Mims may not be aware that Iceland has the highest rate of labor union membership of any country in the world. A total of 91 percent of its workforce is unionized. In an environment *blanketed* with worker-organization I'm fairly certain that no supervisor could ask anyone to continue to work around a corpse without triggering a walkout (and maybe a national scandal). But maybe the core of Mims' point is correct and we should give Amazon the benefit of the doubt that these examples are unrepresentative. At the very least, we should balance them against Mims' own Amazon stories, which will doubtless put the company in a better light.

Let's see!

I am writing this on July 15—Amazon Prime Day, one of the busiest days of the year on the Amazon calendar. I put in a six-hour shift this morning at the West Sacramento warehouse. The workday wasn't brutal. The company treated us all to a pancake breakfast in the break room during our 10-minute break. Of course, you can't eat a pancake breakfast healthily in 10 minutes, but no one in charge complained about the fact that most of us spent at least 20 minutes eating. Yes, we were all encouraged to chant Prime Day slogans during our morning stretch. And we were all given little "Amazon Prime 2019" lapel pins and other bits of "flair" to wear on our high-visibility safety vests. So what? A bit of company spirit is downright American. I don't mind being a small cog in the machinery of American commerce. It keeps the bills paid and my stomach from growling.

...except that it apparently *doesn't* keep the bills paid. Here's what he says as he wraps up his case:

Amazon is not a perfect employer. I have a litany of gripes I'd be happy to share with you sometime. But I also have complaints about the small bookstore I work at in the evenings. I don't know of anyone who doesn't have complaints about their employer.

Got that? He *also* has complaints about the other business where he has to work at nights because his gig at Amazon doesn't pay the bills. Meanwhile, the founder, CEO, and president of the company, Jeff Bezos, has bragged to the press—he really said this—that he has so much money that "the only way" he can see to spend it all is to "convert" his profits "into space travel."

According to the most recent information I could find, the rate of serious injuries at Amazon fulfillment centers is more than twice the national average for the warehousing industry—9.6 injuries per 100 full-time workers in 2018, while the industry average for that year was 4. At least some of those are debilitating back injuries caused by a lot of rapid-fire squatting and lifting as Amazon "associates" race to meet quotas enforced by omnipresent electronic surveillance.

Seeing Mims proudly don his corporate slave collar and do a little dance of appreciation about how Master Bezos is *so generous* that no one at the warehouse was punished for their failure to do the physically impossible thing their supervisors asked them to do—eat a pancake breakfast in 10 minutes without barfing before finishing a shift of literally back-breaking labor—should be enough to make the most hardened cynic look away in embarrassment. But let's slow down and take another look at this business about "gripes."

Mims has complaints about Amazon and complaints about the independent bookstore. Fair enough. Liberals romanticize small business, but leftists know better. Owners of relatively small firms are often the worst workplace tyrants, since they're (justifiably) terrified of being run into the ground by deeper-pocketed competitors and the owners themselves are often in a position to personally micromanage everyone who works for them. Mims' conclusion seems to be that any complaint that applies to *both* businesses must be empty "griping," like complaining about the weather. But that's only true if we assume that the overall relationship between employers and employees baked into the structure of our economic system is "natural" and unchangeable.

It's not. Before capitalism, there was feudalism—which itself emerged from slave-based societies like the Roman Empire—and whether we end up with some form of socialism or a climate-change-fueled collapse into Mad Max barbarism, *something* new will replace capitalism sooner or later. Figuring out what a better society might look like and how we can get there is a complicated and difficult project, but if the best the reactionaries at *Quillette* can do by way of defending the current system is to trot out a spiritually beaten-down sad sack like Kevin Mims to do his sad shuffling slave dance, that should give our side all the confidence in the world that we can win the argument.

But we can't win if we don't play. Every time leftists hold back from entering ideologically hostile media spaces for fear of "legitimizing" our hosts we're throwing away an opportunity to make our case to people who've never heard it before. Every time we go along with "platforming" taboos that discourage leftists from debating reactionaries we're forfeiting the game in the eyes of persuadable onlookers. The real-world effect of acting this way is to hand a propaganda gift to the right. We need to be smarter.

CULTURE, SOCIETY & POLITICS

The modern world is at an impasse. Disasters scroll across our smartphone screens and we're invited to like, follow or upvote, but critical thinking is harder and harder to find. Rather than connecting us in common struggle and debate, the internet has sped up and deepened a long-standing process of alienation and atomization. Zer0 Books wants to work against this trend. With critical theory as our jumping off point, we aim to publish books that make our readers uncomfortable. We want to move beyond received opinions.

Zer0 Books is on the left and wants to reinvent the left. We are sick of the injustice, the suffering and the stupidity that defines both our political and cultural world, and we aim to find a new foundation for a new struggle.

If this book has helped you to clarify an idea, solve a problem or extend your knowledge, you may want to check out our online content as well. Look for Zer0 Books: Advancing Conversations in the iTunes directory and for our Zer0 Books YouTube channel.

Popular videos include:

Žižek and the Double Blackmain

The Intellectual Dark Web is a Bad Sign

Can there be an Anti-SJW Left?

Answering Jordan Peterson on Marxism

Follow us on Facebook
at https://www.facebook.com/ZeroBooks and Twitter at https://
twitter.com/Zer0Books

Bestsellers from Zer0 Books include:

Give Them An Argument
Logic for the Left
Ben Burgis
Many serious leftists have learned to distrust talk of logic. This is
a serious mistake.
Paperback: 978-1-78904-210-8 ebook: 978-1-78904-211-5

Poor but Sexy
Culture Clashes in Europe East and West
Agata Pyzik
How the East stayed East and the West stayed West.
Paperback: 978-1-78099-394-2 ebook: 978-1-78099-395-9

An Anthropology of Nothing in Particular
Martin Demant Frederiksen
A journey into the social lives of meaninglessness.
Paperback: 978-1-78535-699-5 ebook: 978-1-78535-700-8

Cartographies of the Absolute
Alberto Toscano, Jeff Kinkle
An aesthetics of the economy for the twenty-first century.
Paperback: 978-1-78099-275-4 ebook: 978-1-78279-973-3

Malign Velocities
Accelerationism and Capitalism
Benjamin Noys
Long listed for the Bread and Roses Prize 2015, *Malign Velocities*
argues against the need for speed, tracking acceleration
as the symptom of the ongoing crises of capitalism.
Paperback: 978-1-78279-300-7 ebook: 978-1-78279-299-4

Meat Market
Female Flesh under Capitalism
Laurie Penny
A feminist dissection of women's bodies as the fleshy fulcrum of
capitalist cannibalism, whereby women are both consumers and
consumed.
Paperback: 978-1-84694-521-2 ebook: 978-1-84694-782-7

Babbling Corpse
Vaporwave and the Commodification of Ghosts
Grafton Tanner
Paperback: 978-1-78279-759-3 ebook: 978-1-78279-760-9

New Work New Culture
Work we want and a culture that strengthens us
Frithjoff Bergmann
A serious alternative for mankind and the planet.
Paperback: 978-1-78904-064-7 ebook: 978-1-78904-065-4

Romeo and Juliet in Palestine
Teaching Under Occupation
Tom Sperlinger
Life in the West Bank, the nature of pedagogy and the role of a
university under occupation.
Paperback: 978-1-78279-637-4 ebook: 978-1-78279-636-7

Ghosts of My Life
Writings on Depression, Hauntology and Lost Futures
Mark Fisher
Paperback: 978-1-78099-226-6 ebook: 978-1-78279-624-4

Sweetening the Pill
or How We Got Hooked on Hormonal Birth Control
Holly Grigg-Spall
Has contraception liberated or oppressed women?
Sweetening the Pill breaks the silence on the dark side of hormonal
contraception.
Paperback: 978-1-78099-607-3 ebook: 978-1-78099-608-0

Why Are We The Good Guys?
Reclaiming Your Mind from the Delusions of Propaganda
David Cromwell
A provocative challenge to the standard ideology that Western
power is a benevolent force in the world.
Paperback: 978-1-78099-365-2 ebook: 978-1-78099-366-9

The Writing on the Wall
On the Decomposition of Capitalism and its Critics
Anselm Jappe, Alastair Hemmens
A new approach to the meaning of social emancipation.
Paperback: 978-1-78535-581-3 ebook: 978-1-78535-582-0

Enjoying It
Candy Crush and Capitalism
Alfie Bown
A study of enjoyment and of the enjoyment of studying. Bown
asks what enjoyment says about us and what we say about
enjoyment, and why.
Paperback: 978-1-78535-155-6 ebook: 978-1-78535-156-3

Color, Facture, Art and Design
Iona Singh
This materialist definition of fine-art develops guidelines for
architecture, design, cultural-studies and ultimately social
change.
Paperback: 978-1-78099-629-5 ebook: 978-1-78099-630-1

Neglected or Misunderstood
The Radical Feminism of Shulamith Firestone
Victoria Margree
An interrogation of issues surrounding gender, biology,
sexuality, work and technology, and the ways in which our
imaginations continue to be in thrall to ideologies of maternity
and the nuclear family.
Paperback: 978-1-78535-539-4 ebook: 978-1-78535-540-0

How to Dismantle the NHS in 10 Easy Steps (Second Edition)
Youssef El-Gingihy
The story of how your NHS was sold off and why you will have
to buy private health insurance soon. A new expanded second
edition with chapters on junior doctors' strikes and government
blueprints for US-style healthcare.
Paperback: 978-1-78904-178-1 ebook: 978-1-78904-179-8

Digesting Recipes
The Art of Culinary Notation
Susannah Worth
A recipe is an instruction, the imperative tone of the expert, but
this constraint can offer its own kind of potential. A recipe need
not be a domestic trap but might instead offer escape – something
to fantasise about or aspire to.
Paperback: 978-1-78279-860-6 ebook: 978-1-78279-859-0

Most titles are published in paperback and as an ebook.
Paperbacks are available in traditional bookshops. Both print and
ebook formats are available online.
Follow us on Facebook
at https://www.facebook.com/ZeroBooks
and Twitter at https://twitter.com/Zer0Books